A New Canon

A New Canon

*Designing Culturally Sustaining
Humanities Curriculum*

Evan C. Gutierrez

HARVARD EDUCATION PRESS
CAMBRIDGE, MASSACHUSETTS

Paperback ISBN 978-1-68253-601-8
Library Edition ISBN 978-1-68253-602-5

Library of Congress Cataloging-in-Publication Data is on file.

Published by Harvard Education Press,
an imprint of the Harvard Education Publishing Group
Harvard Education Press
8 Story Street
Cambridge, MA 02138

Cover Design: Wilcox Design
Cover Image: petekarici/E+ via Getty Images

The typeface in this book is Adobe Caslon Pro.

Contents

Introduction

I began the work of designing culturally sustaining curriculum, and supporting others to do so, in 2014 when I was an administrator for a network of public charter schools called Acero Schools (previously UNO Charter School Network) in Chicago. I oversaw curriculum and assessment for sixteen schools serving students in grades K–12. The network had been started almost twenty years earlier by Latino community organizers to address overcrowded and underresourced district schools in Latino communities in Chicago. The schools had a solid reputation in the community and were well regarded in the city for driving academic achievement. During my time there, the network was the top-performing charter organization according to the city's School Quality Rating Policy.

While Acero had an impressive "for us, by us" ethos, that character was not yet showing up in the academic program. Acero parents took ownership of the schools, and network leadership could easily mobilize them. There were arts and music offerings (including a particularly impressive mariachi program) that honored the culture and heritage of the people who had built the network. The schools were named for Latinx authors, poets, and leaders, but students did not learn about them. While the students came primarily from Latino households and many spoke Spanish at home, the curriculum on balance was fairly traditional—especially in the humanities, where kids studied traditional Anglo-centric topics in history and literature. Much of my work, therefore, was organized to integrate the ethos and ideals of the organization into the academic program. I worked

1

with leaders across the organization to design equity into the academic program, such that students would be able to leverage their full set of cultural and linguistic assets in their academic pursuits.

At about this time the state of Illinois began the process of adopting new social studies standards based on the C3 (College, Career and Civic Life) Framework for Social Studies State Standards established by the National Council for the Social Studies in 2010. These new standards would be content agnostic—a departure from the state's existing standards, which articulated a list of historical events and characters that students would learn about. The focus instead would be on building a set of skills to guide historians, economists, geographers, and engaged citizens. The new standards would not come with a prescribed curriculum. Early conversations at the state level suggested that schools might design curriculum using the C3 Framework as a guide.

The move away from a prescriptive set of social studies standards created an opportunity for Acero to adopt a curriculum that represented the community we served. That there was policy to support the ideal future state—one where students from the Latino community could consistently study the histories and narratives of people who looked like them, had similar experiences, faced similar challenges, and enjoyed similar triumphs—was electrifying.

Summer after summer, I brought together a group of instructional leaders and teachers representing various schools and grade levels to create standards maps using the new framework. We also discussed our plans and possible next steps. We imagined finding a social studies or humanities curriculum that would cultivate students' sense of belonging and enfranchisement through an ever-deepening knowledge of Latino activists, artists, authors, and civil servants.

As we moved from mapping to looking for resources, however, our enthusiasm was dampened. There were few existing texts that centered the Latino experience in the way that we envisioned. This came as a surprise. Available resources focused only on activism or times when Latino issues became national news, falling short of the fuller expression of community life that we'd hoped for. These seemed to have been created with the general public in mind, not for Latinos seeking to deepen their knowledge of their own histories. While there were some curricula from a previous era, when the civil rights movement had resulted in a push for ethnic studies to be offered in public schools, these materials were not aligned with current thinking about social studies education. New pedagogies organized around inquiry and application in the world outside of school were not reflected in those materials. They were fundamentally built on a different template than all current curriculum.

We decided that if no curriculum yet existed, we would adapt and implement a framework for designing curriculum that would reflect the identity of our community. But while many frameworks for curriculum design were available, none of them gave any significant weight to cultural relevance or guidance for how to design curriculum for students from marginalized communities. There was simply nothing available.

This, too, came as a shock. Many of us had read Friere, Ladson-Billings, and Gay in our preservice training. Django Paris's call for a culturally sustaining pedagogy "to perpetuate and foster—to sustain—linguistic, literate, and cultural pluralism as part of the democratic project of schooling" was so clear and resonant. Certainly we were not the only educators serving in communities of color, seeking to have the character of our community alive in our classrooms as these scholars had inspired us to do. I had been prepared to build consensus on a plan for cultural relevance, purchase materials, and support their use. Plan B was to implement an existing framework for designing culturally relevant curriculum and support its use. But there was no such curriculum, and there were no guide books for designing one.

To build a culturally sustaining curriculum for our students, I leaned on previous professional experience as a curriculum designer and facilitator of curriculum development. Past work had allowed me to bring educators together with content experts to design new courses of study. These included single courses, programs for multiple schools in a district or network of schools, and whole-school models. The foci ranged from entrepreneurship to digital journalism to arts integration. I'd had success with this recipe. When the process created opportunities for educators to bring their classroom-based expertise and subject-matter experts to bring their field-based knowledge to bear, the final product reflected the best of both.

When all went well, those programs worked in real-world classrooms and engaged students in practices that were authentic to the field: entrepreneurship looked and felt more like what entrepreneurs actually do; digital journalism was patterned on current practices, not outdated or watered-down "newsroom activities."

As colleagues we decided that our students were worth the risk of entering into a design process that we could find no guideposts for. Because there was no guide, we did not know if what we produced would land. We did not know if others would criticize it. We were unsure of how much use it would get. All of these uncertainties weighed on us, but they were preferable to the alternative. Having done our due diligence, we knew that the alternative was a totally unacceptable reality in which students had zero opportunities to authentically study the histories of their community via the formal curriculum. Even if what we produced was not perfect, we were convinced to move forward. We could analyze our own efficacy against very simple criteria: students in grades 6–12 would have x opportunities to study Latinx history, y opportunities to read Latinx authors, and z classroom examinations of *testimonio* from their community. These efforts and their willingness to confront the cognitive dissonance presented by the work ahead were worthwhile, as x, y, z would ultimately represent a greater value than their current values of *seldom*, *maybe in college*, and *never*, respectively.

I developed a design process that included significant research and discovery, peer review for alignment with standards, and consultation with an expert. Dr. Héctor García Chávez, who chaired the Latino Studies Department at Loyola University Chicago, agreed to meet with us, offer perspective on the work, and provide resources from his personal library. Each step of the design process was organized to authentically reflect Latinx scholars' thinking and interpretation of their history and literature. The work of the educators was to "curricularize" that perspective such that teachers across our network of schools could implement it.

Each school had a schedule that worked for it. Most allocated more time to English language arts (ELA) than to social studies. Each staff was different: the teachers who would embrace a culturally sustaining curriculum did not all teach the same subject or grade level. We wanted to give this curriculum the best possible chance to be implemented well, and the maximum possible number of teachers the opportunity to use it and offer feedback. To that end, the curriculum that we designed was modular and interdisciplinary. It was modular in the sense that these projects could be brought into an existing course, and the teacher could choose where in the sequence they would fit best. Some teachers combined multiple projects to create an elective. The curriculum was interdisciplinary in that it referenced history, literature, and civic engagement. Seasoned language arts teachers could use their well-developed instructional muscle to teach this curriculum in an ELA course. Social studies teachers similarly could see the curriculum's natural fit in their classes due to its history and civics focus.

Since this first endeavor I have run multiple design cohorts with educators from across the country. These engagements have typically been sponsored by an organization that has identified culturally sustaining curriculum as an unmet need in its community, and have ranged from day-long design sprints to remote experiences spanning months. Originally designed to support the development of curriculum centered on the Latinx intellectual tradition, the process has been reused and repurposed. Designers in subsequent cohorts have used the same process to design curriculum centered on other intellectual traditions that have been excluded from typical academic programs. Professionals including teachers, school leaders, curriculum designers, and nonprofit and community leaders have taken that on. They have been inspired by the same desire for their students to be cultivated in their own intellectual tradition, sometimes unwilling to tolerate the erasure that they themselves experienced in their schooling. Professionals using this process for curriculum design come from many states, two dozen at this time, and inquiries or units that have been produced through this process are being implemented in forty-three states.

Educators who have used this process to design curriculum have produced not only useful materials, but also a change in mind-set. The process itself is educative, allowing for previously nebulous ideas about equity in education to become tangible. Mary O'Brien-Combs, a designer in the 2018 cohort, described this shift as impacting not only her understanding of curriculum, but also her aims as an educator:

> For the past several years, I've approached teaching with a grave sense of urgency, intensely concerned with fully arming students with everything

they'll need to navigate a dismissive higher-education system. Through the process of collaboration, discussion, and exploration of resources as part of this project, my view has shifted. I now no longer feel I have to coach my students on the quickest way to get around a sleeping ogre, but to instead pause, focus, and take a thoughtful aim in learning about their own inherently spectacular legacy of strength.

Educators who use these materials in their classrooms tend to increase their use semester over semester, year over year. Where a teacher has used one project in a given semester, they are likely to use two the next. Where a teacher has used two to three over the course of a year, they are likely to create a semester-long elective the next. Designers like Ericka Streeter-Adams, from the 2018 and 2019 cohorts, describe dramatic changes in their students' engagement and investment, taking pride in and ownership of their learning:

> From the onset you could see the curiosity arise in my scholars' eyes and the pride they exude knowing and feeling connected to the discourse. As opposed to students being the audience of a stale and stagnant lecture, within this curricular paradigm they have become the "experts," leveraging their cultural insight, awareness, and wonderings. The scholars value the discussions, and the tasks have taken on a new life. The conversational tone has become more universal and relevant, and owned by each individual scholar. In this culturally equitable environment we have leveraged the community of thinkers. It feels like a cultural and academic rebirth.

Regardless of their role or level of expertise in curriculum design, I refer to these professionals, while they are engaged in this process, as "designers." While you are driving, you are considered a driver. Likewise, while engaged in design the teachers, nonprofit leaders, instructional leaders, and community members who take on this work are designers. This book is intended to guide the reader through this process of discovery, creative struggle, and shrewd decision-making as designers.

Designers, welcome.

About the Book

The purpose of this book is to provide the rationale and step-by-step guidance that teachers and school leaders, working with scholars and others, can use to produce rigorous, standards-aligned, culturally sustaining humanities units. Modular in nature, these units can be used as part of an existing course or in combination to create new courses for middle and high school students.

I call the units produced by this framework "culturally sustaining" because I believe they are consistent with Django Paris's use of this term in the 2012 essay where he coined it. Paris posited that today's scholars and practitioners may stand on the shoulders of the scholars who gave us culturally relevant and responsive pedagogies in order to go further:[1]

> Recently, however, I have begun to question if the terms "relevant" and "responsive" are really descriptive of much of the teaching and research founded upon them and, more importantly, if they go far enough in their orientation to the languages and literacies and other cultural practices of communities marginalized by systemic inequalities to ensure the valuing and maintenance of our multiethnic and multilingual society. In this essay, I offer the term and stance of "culturally sustaining pedagogy" as an alternative that, I believe, embodies some of the best research and practice in the resource pedagogy tradition and as a term that supports the value of our multiethnic and multilingual present and future. Culturally sustaining pedagogy seeks to perpetuate and foster—to sustain—linguistic, literate, and cultural pluralism as part of the democratic project of schooling. In the face of current policies and practices that have the explicit goal of creating a monocultural and monolingual society, research and practice need equally explicit resistances that embrace cultural pluralism and cultural equality.

This book is intended to operationalize Paris's culturally sustaining pedagogy as the Inquiry Design Model did for inquiry-based teaching and project-based learning did for constructivism. When practitioners make powerful educational philosophy and pedagogies operational (with tools, products, and step-by-step processes), powerful things happen. Communities of practice come together. There are tangible tools that change the daily educational experience of teachers and students. There are products that can be critiqued and improved upon through iteration.

I have organized the book into three parts. Part I introduces the "why" and "what" of the new canon and places the work in a historical, methodological, and pedagogical context. Part II is devoted to the sequential steps involved in building culturally sustaining curriculum units. The final section, Part III, provides educators with tools to successfully integrate these units into the context of their courses, schools, and communities in a way that, in Paris's words, "supports the value of our multiethnic and multilingual present and future."

The process presented in this book has been practiced by many, revised, remixed, and codified. The steps can be taken in as little as two weeks or as long as three months, depending on the needs and obligations of the designers. These steps are in no way easy, but, if they are followed, the results are transformative. The steps are organized to apply the designers' attention to the cultural relevance and authenticity of each design decision. The product should be a project or unit of study that authentically represents the intellectual tradition of the community that it is being written for. An LGBTQ+ project should examine parts of that experience from the LGBTQ+ perspective. A project about Muslim American literature will ask the questions Muslim American authors struggle with. A unit on Chicano muralists might ask students to propose a mural design that demonstrates deep knowledge of that artistic tradition.

Each design step is preceded by a discussion of its theoretical basis. This includes a description of the scholarship to support why the design step might differ from common practices in curriculum design and research on ways that common practices and the formal curriculum have failed students in marginalized communities. These sections presume that most readers have had either professional or personal experiences of the K–12 schooling system that have ingrained in them ideas and beliefs that need to be confronted. This is not an indictment of the designer, but a recognition of the ways that the system of schooling has systematically marginalized the histories and narratives of nondominant communities. Where designers seek to create something different than has been available in the past, they cannot employ past methods. And in order to do something new—something that for many will feel uncomfortable or nonintuitive—most of us need to know *why* we are doing something new.

Design steps are followed by examples of real designers who have used the process described in this book to create projects for their own use and to be used by others. I'll also describe the challenges these designers faced and the decisions they made. Readers will see the way that their projects evolved step by step. The designers demonstrate that even with different themes and content, the process produces resources that have shared qualities and character. The project maps they produced are introduced in the chapters, and their final published curricular units are shared in their entirety in the appendixes and are also freely available as open educational resources.

These designers were participants in a design cohort in early 2019 sponsored by Gradient Learning (the organization that runs the Summit Learning Program) and C3Teachers, a community of teachers and teacher educators engaged in using inquiry in social studies education. Both organizations involved their leaders in planning, facilitating, and reviewing the projects that were produced. The projects that are featured in this book as examples, along with others, are available at no cost to partner schools on the Summit Learning Platform, and to the general public on C3teachers .org.

It is important to stress that the designers featured in this book all have different roles in their respective organizations. Each entered into the process having a unique motivation and seeking to write for a distinct community. I included a variety of designers intentionally in the hopes that readers will be able to see ways they can use their own particular expertise and assets to engage in the design process. These designers include the following:

Malika Ali is the Director of Pedagogy for The Highlander Institute, where she develops programs to support culturally sustaining and responsive pedagogy, instructional equity, and innovation for schools throughout New England. Malika's engagement with the design cohort was inspired by a desire to build skills in curriculum design and also to produce resources that would resonate with students in the Eritrean and Ethiopian community where she lives in Providence, Rhode Island. She is a former Rhode Island Teacher of the Year, having taught STEM subjects in Providence Public Schools. Malika identifies as the daughter of strong and brilliant Eritrean refugees.

Cameron (Cam) Lloyd is a Lead Curriculum Designer for EL Education, a national education nonprofit that provides curriculum, professional development, and support to schools nationwide. Cam works on a large curriculum team, building capacity in team members and developing resources relating to accessibility and intervention. He worked as an elementary school teacher and reading specialist in Washington, DC, New York, and Seattle before shifting to full-time program development. Cam was motivated to participate in the design cohort in part to develop his facility with curriculum development to augment his expertise in literacy programming. Cam was also inspired to fill a gap that he saw in upper elementary school curriculum addressing LGBTQ identity.

David Alfafara is the Assistant Principal for Curriculum and Instruction at Victoria Soto High School in Chicago's Gage Park neighborhood. David oversees a large staff and is responsible for professional development, curriculum, and instruction for a school serving predominantly Latinx and Black students. David has taught and had leadership roles in a variety of charter schools in Chicago following a successful career in business. David's engagement with the design cohort was inspired by his knowledge of ways that the formal curriculum fails to address the experiences of the Black and brown students in urban schools.

Annabeth Edens is the Social Studies Department Chair and teacher at Royal Spring Middle School outside Lexington, Kentucky. Annabeth has consistently engaged in curriculum development in her practice, led design efforts in her school, and served on advisory boards for the state. She is committed to culturally responsive teaching practices and deeply familiar with inquiry-based design. Annabeth was engaged with this design cohort to continue to build her capacity for curriculum design, and particularly to grow in her ability to design with a focus on equity and with her African American students in mind.

How to Use This Book

There are a few ways individuals, school-based teams, or multischool teams might use this book and the associated materials. The first potential use is to follow the steps and design projects. In this case, the design process will familiarize the individual or group with the theory and pedagogy that undergirds these projects. That familiarity will enable the use not only of the projects they design, but also of projects designed by others using this process. Designers might then add to or build new courses using both types of projects.

The second potential use is to read the book solely to become familiar with the pedagogy and design principles in order to implement projects designed by others. In this case, there may be a core group designing new projects and an additional group using the book to prepare them to teach those projects. Individuals may read the book, prepare and teach existing projects, and use that experience to design their own projects at a later time.

The wrong approach would be reading this book with the notion that groups or individuals will need to create all their own projects. That idea is both daunting and runs counter to the spirit of this work. If we are to build a body of work sufficient to constitute a new canon of curriculum that better reflects our students, we must rely on one another and engage in this work as a community. So, if you plan read this book in order to design projects, know that others have gone before and their work is available to you for reference or inspiration. If you plan to read this book in order to prepare to teach projects, know that there are good projects readily available to you. This work began as a community effort, and you are invited to engage with the work in that same spirit—as a member of an ever-growing community.

I

Setting the Stage for a New Canon

CHAPTER I

Establishing "Why"

The Need for a New Canon

S tudents come from communities, and communities belong to an intellectual tradition. A community's intellectual tradition is made up of
histories, literature, philosophy, and more. Thinkers, writers, and notable
figures across generations pour their efforts, creativity, and wisdom into a
pool of ideas that future generations will draw on.

There is a Black intellectual tradition. Black historians refer to one another's works; Black poets borrow and develop techniques from the authors
that went before. There is a Jewish intellectual tradition. It is rooted in
thousands of years of scholarship—ways of asking questions, and questions
about questions. There is a Latino intellectual tradition where layered mes-
tizo language and vibrant imagery have characterized creative writing for
generations. There is an LGBTQ intellectual tradition, where the particularity of queerness connects politicians and advocates across time and space.

It is good to be close to the deep and broad pool that makes up the
intellectual tradition of the community one comes from. One can see one's

own image reflected on the pool's surface. The connection to great thinkers, with similar challenges or triumphs, can be nourishing and sustaining. To be cultivated first in one's own intellectual tradition is essentially human.

To be cultivated in the intellectual tradition of one's community of origin allows for students to draw on their home- and community-based resources. A community's intellectual tradition has a canon all its own, made of history, literature, and aesthetics. Students will read authors with surnames like theirs, refer to quotes or colloquialisms that their parents are familiar with, learn history their grandparents might speak to firsthand. When a person is cultivated in the intellectual tradition of their community, their home- and community-based knowledge becomes an asset they can use in their schooling. Such assets might include language and vocabulary, familiarity with topics and ideas, or skills they've practiced that are useful in their schooling. Being able to draw on these assets builds agency and confidence for students, and allows them to learn more quickly and deeply. Unfortunately, this advantage is currently made available to White middle-class students, and not others.

The curriculum is organized to cultivate students in the intellectual tradition of the dominant group. The historical narratives and literature that make up the canon of humanities curriculum in US public schools privilege White voices. These accounts underrepresent the perspectives, histories, and literature from communities of color.[1] For students who are White, this is a significant yet somehow invisible and unacknowledged advantage.[2] For students who are not White, their schooling takes the form of an extended onboarding to an intellectual tradition not their own. These students will spend thirteen years learning about writers, historical figures, music, how to communicate, and how to make sense of the world like a person from a different culture. Their home-based knowledge will be varying degrees of useless. As they enter the doors of the school building, their home-based intellectual assets will trade for sixty cents on the dollar.

Some are very comfortable with the idea that school's purpose and duty is to bring these students on, to teach them the skills and ways of being that will help them to be successful in the dominant culture. After all, this is the definition of success, is it not? Wouldn't we be leaving students in the lurch if they were not equipped with the tools they need to succeed in the world of the gringo? Schools did not create the disparities, and the only realistic goal is to teach students to navigate them.

Others are quite uncomfortable with this type of systemic inequity. If we are supporting public schools, shouldn't the schooling match the public? Is it not right for our models and aims to evolve as our student body becomes increasingly diverse? As we understand more clearly the effects of cultural erasure? If we want to run public and decolonized schools, the goal must be for students to have access to and be cultivated in their own intellectual tradition.

Educators, through their actions, will make one of the preceding paradigms true for their students. Regardless of what educators may believe is *really true* about the world, it will be their choices that determine whether a student may access or is cultivated in their own intellectual tradition. Where educators believe that onboarding is necessary, students will not have access to their intellectual tradition for the time they are in that classroom. Their home- and community-based assets will be all but useless. Where educators are motivated to address inequities, their efforts will enable students to leverage their assets, to see and touch that deep pool and be filled up by it. For educators who choose this latter path, the arrow that has been missing from our collective quiver is a culturally sustaining curriculum.

The Problem with Traditional Curriculum

Gloria Ladson-Billings, in her seminal article *Toward a Theory of Culturally Relevant Pedagogy* (1995), argued: "A next step for positing effective pedagogical practice is a theoretical model that not only addresses student achievement but also helps students to accept and affirm their cultural identity while developing critical perspectives that challenge inequities that schools (and other institutions) perpetuate."[3]

This and related work to follow were focused on teacher practice, observing the work of effective teachers of children of color, and surfacing practice that could inform others, particularly those involved in teacher education. In this and other texts, Ladson-Billings points to the deficiencies in the traditional curriculum. In a 2003 article, "Lies My Teacher Still Tells: Developing a Critical Race Perspective Toward the Social Studies," she states, "If one were to attempt to construct the history of African

Americans based on the information presented in a typical U.S. History textbook, that history might consist of the following" and proceeds to articulate historical events spanning from the colonial period to the present, amounting to a short paragraph.[4]

Geneva Gay, author of *Culturally Responsive Teaching* (2000) and a number of hallmark resources for preparing teachers to work effectively in multicultural contexts, has a similar assessment of the traditional curriculum. In *Preparing for Culturally Responsive Teaching* (2002), Gay says the following about formal school curricula's treatment of ethnic diversity:

> There are several recurrent trends in how formal school curricula deal with ethnic diversity that culturally responsive teachers need to correct. Among them are avoiding controversial issues such as racism, historical atrocities, powerlessness, and hegemony; focusing on the accomplishments of the same few high-profile individuals repeatedly and ignoring the actions of groups; giving proportionally more attention to African Americans than other groups of color; decontextualizing women, their issues, and their actions from their race and ethnicity; ignoring poverty; and emphasizing factual information while minimizing other kinds of knowledge (such as values, attitudes, feelings, experiences, and ethics).[5]

While Ladson-Billings' and Gay's work has been enormously influential in problematizing the curriculum and offers teachers recommendations on how they might modify it, neither suggests that schools and districts might work toward reducing cultural mismatch by creating or providing culturally sustaining curricula.

The reality of the current state is that the gap between available curriculum and what would be ideal for students is meant to be closed by teachers. This requires additional planning to make connections, new instructional practices to build belonging and connection, sourcing additional materials to create mini-lessons, and more. The field of practice sends the message, "It would be good if there were relevant curriculum for your students, but there are no such materials, so here is what you can do with what *is* available." This message perfectly mirrors that sent to students who are not part of the dominant group, that "this system was not created with you in mind, but if you put in the extra effort, through tenacity and ingenuity you may be able to get to *good enough*."

In recent years, Ladson-Billings has suggested that even while her work is widely cited, those involved in bringing research to practice have managed to implement only a shallow notion of cultural relevance, dulling its essential critical edge and instead adding superficial cultural examples and analogues as they teach prescribed curricula.[6]

I believe that to be a fair assessment. The dominant interpretations of these frameworks are enormously reductive and run entirely counter to their ethos and purpose. Common interpretations are intended to make cultural relevance approachable and defined in terms that would allow for a broader group to believe that they have been successful in incorporating these theories.

One such interpretation is that "it's not about the picture, it's about the frame." This suggests that the culturally responsive teachers' work is to frame traditional content for students in a way that will engage them, activating their home-based knowledge to allow them to more quickly access the traditional curriculum.

Another common interpretation is that cultural relevance is about using students' interests to "hook" them into engagement with the traditional curriculum. Examples include referencing music or sports and using vernacular to make students more receptive to learning what is in the textbooks.[7]

Setting aside my belief that these are disingenuous interpretations of the available scholarship and literature, both suggest that there was never anything wrong with the curriculum in the first place. These interpretations are fully situated within the onboarding paradigm, affirming adherents in their belief that the gap between the dominant ideologies presented in school and the experiences of students from nondominant groups are for the students to close. Culturally responsive teachers, out of the goodness of their hearts, will help them close that gap, but the gap is because of the students' deficiency, not the school's.

The effects that this paradigm has on students are both negative and dire. Angela Valenzuela extends the notion of "subtractive" practice from sociolinguistic literature, where language education subtracts one's original language and culture, to a number of school-based practices and structures.[8] She describes marginalization in the formal curriculum, stripping

students of their cultural markers (by butchering Spanish-language surnames, for example), and discounting or rejecting students' academic ca-
pacities (e.g., previous academic achievements, language proficiency). The
cumulative effect is an erosion of students' social capital and what I term
academic disenfranchisement. Where this paradigm is in play, students are
taught things they already know as if they don't know them. Black history
and literature are taught from a White perspective. The Spanish language
is taught to heritage speakers from an English-dominant, world-language
perspective as though they were starting from scratch. In these environments students pursue academic success at their own expense. While Valenzuela observes these dynamics among Mexican American students,
Ladson-Billings' research also suggests that Black students face similar
challenges. Interacting with this model of academic success is at cross-
purposes with students' developing cultural competence.[9] The nonsubtle
message to (particularly Black and Latinx) students is that "the *you* that
God made, that your parents named, must change in order to be good."
Small wonder that when schools require students to divest in their whole
selves, many students choose to divest in school.

Beyond "Wokeness": The Need for New Resources

The challenges presented by the deficiencies of the curriculum are unreasonably hard to surmount. Much of the extant literature describes the efforts that individual teachers make to involve community members, revise
and remix curricular resources, or build courses from scratch to meet their
students' needs. The development of good curriculum is no small task, and
the pressure to implement districtwide solutions with fidelity presents a
real threat to those moving forward with classroom-based solutions. Culturally responsive teachers are put in a position to take on a significant
amount of personal responsibility *and* potentially to adopt a posture of
noncompliance regarding implementation of the formal curriculum where
that curriculum is insufficient. Teaching is a hard job, and this layer makes
it close to impossible.

For school and district leaders who are invested in building culturally sustaining learning spaces, noninvestment in the curriculum presents
similar challenges. In my own practice as a leader, I have been frustrated

by solutions that focus solely on changing mind-sets. I have often thought, and sometimes said, "Students' right and access to culturally sustaining learning cannot depend on the wokeness of their teacher alone." Teachers need resources and investment from administrators. Providing training and no tools (i.e., curricular materials) for a nearly impossible task is not a satisfying solution. Districts are increasingly creating comprehensive plans for the adoption of specific curricula, often including measures for the external validation of curriculum. This stems from research substantiating that a high-quality curriculum is a powerful driver for improving student outcomes and that training to the curriculum is more effective than professional development on generalizable principles.[10] These dynamics call into question the long-term effectiveness of a strategy of investing solely in teachers' mind-set.

So what to do? Django Paris, a public intellectual who has extended Ladson-Billings' work into new territory, challenges educators to think about curriculum in a different way. In *Culturally Sustaining Pedagogies* (Teachers College Press, 2017), Paris and his co-editor, H. Samy Alim, argue that educators must *curricularize*—or make into curriculum—core elements of culturally sustaining pedagogies. These include centering community's languages, fostering community agency and input, connecting current lived realities to the storied histories of these communities, and contending with internalized oppressions. Ladson-Billings acknowledges Paris's fresh take on her work, and ways his scholarship presents a next evolution of her framework, in *Culturally Relevant Pedagogy 2.0: The Remix* (2014), writing, "I hope to help those who subscribe to earlier visions of culturally relevant pedagogy make the transition to the remix: culturally sustaining pedagogy."[11]

To effectively curricularize these pedagogies as Paris and Alim describe, leaders of schools, districts, and classrooms must involve themselves in comprehensive solutions and invest in curriculum and pedagogies where "languages, literacies, and cultural ways of being that our students and communities embody" are sustained.[12]

Mutual investment in culturally sustaining curriculum involving district, school, and classroom leaders will anchor and catalyze the transformation that scholars have been urging for more than twenty-five years.

Our espoused values regarding cultural relevance should be evident in our book lists, our course catalogs, and our lesson plans. A failure to curricularize these values places an unreasonable burden on the willing and lets adherents to the onboarding paradigm completely off the hook. A student's access to culturally sustaining pedagogies cannot fall only on woke teachers. It is time for the curriculum to do the heavy lifting.

It Is, Actually, the Curriculum

Our students do indeed know things. All of them, in fact. When classrooms are set up to make use of students' knowledge, students excel. This notion is the central thrust of Luis C. Moll and his coauthors' formation of *funds of knowledge*. Their research confronts the common conception that working-class and culturally nondominant households are "disorganized socially and deficient intellectually."[13] This research points to ample intellectual and cultural resources that students may draw on for academic purposes.

Moll and colleagues' studies have demonstrated that, when educators think first of the information and skills that students have at their disposal and organize academic work with these resources in mind, students and teachers both benefit. Although this research, conducted with families in the border regions between the US and Mexico, was limited in scope to specific elements of home-based knowledge such as agricultural, business, and household management, Moll and coauthors establish a principle that is transferable: when ideas and information that students are familiar with is prioritized in the curriculum, there is a privileging effect. These *privileging effects of familiarity* are at the core of academic enfranchisement or disenfranchisement.

Students from dominant cultural groups benefit consistently from these privileging effects. Students are well served when academic programs leverage their full cultural and linguistic resources. Whiteness is assigned disproportionately high value in the curriculum through emphasis. While there is much to support the notion that this imbalance has a negative effect on the development of positive self-concept for students of color, this is not central to the argument put forth in this book. Rather, the focus is on the privileging effects of interacting with content where characters, sociolect, themes, and ideas are familiar to the student. *If students' interaction with familiar content is a benefit, why not endeavor to provide that benefit to all students?*

If this type of curriculum would have such clear benefits, why are resources that would be familiar to students in nondominant cultural groups so scarce?[14]

The answer is about economics, not pedagogy or sociology. Until quite recently the market dynamics that govern the field of curriculum development would make creation of such materials nonviable. The costs associated with creating a quality curriculum are high enough that textbook producers look to the largest and most stable buyers possible to establish their market. Sometimes referred to as the "Texas effect," this means that a curriculum producer would need to know that their product aligned with the needs of a large market for it to be viable. For example, a history text would have to be marketable to the entire state of Texas (where the state board is authorized to purchase textbooks for all schools) to meet this standard. Content that some constituents might find unpalatable presents a significant conflict. Producers targeting these markets must think about the preferences of their most conservative possible buyer and cater to those preferences.

There is mounting pressure that may affect or change this dynamic. Parent and teacher groups continue to push for changes to the formal curriculum as a way to address the rise in exposed and unapologetic racism in our society. Advocates are beginning to see their demands for action answered as policies to add or require ethnic and gender studies as part of the formal curriculum are increasingly being adopted. Even when state governments and other policy makers recognize the value of academic programs that cohere to students' cultural identities, it is difficult for traditional curriculum providers to meet the needs that new policies create. California passed a law (which has since become optional) requiring that ethnic studies be offered to high school students in that state, leaving the state curriculum board to determine what should be included. That committee has been mired in debate, and has heard arguments from leadership of dozens of ethnic communities requesting representation in that curriculum. As I write this passage, the committee has been unable to navigate these complexities and produce a recommendation that the state superintendent can move forward. How unlikely is it, given market uncertainty, that a curriculum provider would step into the fray and produce the materials necessary for this course?

Still, many states continue to pass instructional mandates requiring that schools teach histories and narratives that traditionally have been excluded from curriculum. During my time working as an administrator in Illinois, the state government passed instructional mandates requiring schools to teach LGBTQ history and address Mexican Repatriation in the 1930s. I was enthusiastic to comply, as I believed that students in my network would benefit. I found nothing available on the market substantively addressing these topics and eventually gave up waiting, deciding instead that our network would create the materials ourselves. I believe that the grain size (a single unit or project for each of those mandates) was far too small for producers to take notice. The potential return would not justify the investment.

When the unit of change is the teacher, their efforts, no matter how earnest, will not produce work substantial enough for change to root. When the unit of change is the curriculum provider, that large ship turns too slowly and is governed by the wrong dynamics to put forth a solution. And so, seventeen years after Gloria Ladson-Billings' indictment of the curriculum, it is still possible and even likely that Black students will graduate from high school knowing fewer than nine facts about Black history. I fear that the prospects are even worse for Latinos, LGBTQ persons, and the many other cultures that make up our student bodies.[15]

A Community Effort

There has been progress toward better representation in texts. Language arts curricula are being produced, particularly by open educational resource (OER) providers, using texts that feature a diversity of non-White protagonists. Publishers of books for K–12 audiences are making progress toward representing the diversity of identities that make up their readership. K–12 book lists (or approved reading lists) are following suit, albeit slowly. Analyses of the diversity (based on race, ethnicity, sexuality, gender identity, and ability) of texts in school and public libraries suggest that institutional investments in this area have not kept pace with the marketplace.[16] Even so, diverse representation in texts is commonly and inappropriately used as a proxy for progress toward culturally sustaining curriculum.

Assigning texts with non-White protagonists is progress, but when weighed against the elements that Paris and Alim suggest should be curricularized, or the standard set up earlier in this chapter for allowing students access to the depth and breadth of the intellectual tradition of their community, it falls short.

Selecting a text is an important decision, but it is only one of several decisions that curriculum designers make. Each of these decisions will be informed by the designer's paradigm and contribute to the students' enfranchisement or the erosion of their cultural identities.

If a student is to access the intellectual tradition of their community, all aspects of the curriculum must authentically reflect that tradition. For that study, students must be seated close to the pool in order to see their reflection, drink from the water, and be nourished by it. Curriculum that describes the pool from a distance does not rise to the standard that scholars have set forth. It is insufficient for students to examine their intellectual tradition from the dominant perspective. What a shame for Black students to learn what non-Black scholars think about Black literature or history. The curriculum, and all of its component parts, should be situated within the intellectual tradition of the community that it is being written for. Students ought not only read texts about Latinx characters, but also be prompted to ask the questions Latinx scholars would ask about that text. Where students might learn about Muslim artists, should the arc of that learning not reflect a deep knowledge of Muslim art? Where a student is invited into learning about their own intellectual tradition, should they not be invited to demonstrate their knowledge in a way that leverages all of their assets?

This might seem like an unreasonably high bar, but it is exactly what is expected of curriculum design in other disciplines. The Next Generation Science Standards are organized such that students not only *learn* science (including facts and principles) but also *do* science. And why? So that students engage with the discipline in a way that authentically reflects adult practice. Common Core Language Arts standards ask that students read, analyze, and write like writers. The C3 Framework for Social Studies State Standards is set up to encourage students to think like economists, historians, and geographers and engage with civics like adults in those fields. Great care is taken to ensure that students engage in these learning experiences in a way that is developmentally appropriate and accessible. Still, authentic engagement with the field of practice is the bar.

It is time for a framework by which culturally sustaining humanities curriculum design can meet this standard, and that is the purpose of this book. Theoretical basis, practical direction, and object lessons taken from the field are provided for each of the major processes designers must execute to build this curriculum. These processes are ordered to allow for discovery, research, and expert consultation at critical junctures. This is in acknowledgment of the fact that many designers who will engage in this work will begin with a limited understanding of the intellectual tradition of the community they are writing for.

The result should be projects that can be implemented by designers and shared with colleagues, and that are modular enough in nature that the arrangement of these materials can be decided locally.

Cultural relevance need not come down to individual teachers. And communities need not wait for traditional providers of curriculum to meet this need. It will be communities made up of scholars, educators, administrators, and families who answer the decades-old call for a culturally sustaining curriculum. Students and families will have more opportunities to sit by the pool created by the knowledge and genius of their forebears.

So let's begin.

CHAPTER 2

Describing "What"

Projects for Building a New Canon

This chapter offers an overview of what is to be designed in the new curriculum. Specifically, this chapter will introduce the four core components that make up a culturally sustaining humanities unit: an authentic question, final demonstration of knowledge, sources, and formative tasks. This chapter will also illustrate how to organize these components to produce a unit that can be shared. The importance of adopting a designer's mind-set and considering how the units can be adapted in a local context will also be addressed.

What Will Be Designed

The output of this design process is meant to look and feel like projects in a project-based learning (PBL) frame. Thus, the structure and style will be familiar to those working in PBL environments or implementing such projects as a supplement to traditional curriculum. PBL structures have much in common with inquiries (drawn from inquiry-based instruction) and problems (from problem-based learning). Components in these frameworks have different names and are associated with distinct pedagogies, but serve similar structural purposes.

Essential questions, driving questions, problems, and *compelling questions* serve as the organizing question for a unit, project, or inquiry within these various frameworks. Students explore multiple perspectives on or solutions to the organizing question through a set of narrower, more specific questions. These narrower questions generally are supported by primary and secondary sources, grouped to enable the completion of formative tasks. Completion of these formative tasks equips the students with knowledge or skills that allow them to respond to the organizing question comprehensively, solve the problem, or propose a solution. In our work building culturally sustaining humanities units, we call the organizing question for the project the *authentic question.* This term is a cue for the designer that the question must be *authentic to* the intellectual tradition of the community they are writing for.

The pedagogies associated with the various frameworks just mentioned are also different. The way that the organizing questions are composed, the nature of the grouped resources, the associated formative assessments, and the students' summative demonstration of knowledge are distinct and worthy of individual examination. In their guiding principles and format, however, the products of these frameworks are quite similar. This commonality in format between these other frameworks and the one described in this book is intentional. The similarity advantages teachers and instructional leaders using this design process and increases the resulting projects' digestibility by other educators. Users in many contexts will be familiar with the format, if not the content and pedagogy. Curriculum and instructional designers need to consider the needs not only of their students but also of teachers, particularly if the materials they are designing are intended to be used in other classrooms. The designer can leverage users' previous experience and expertise—that is, what they know and have done before—in order to introduce something new. Maintaining familiar structures prevents extraneous cognitive load on the teacher, allowing for more attention to be allocated to new pedagogy and content.[1] It also enables teachers to draw on their previous experience and long-term memory, which frees up cognitive resources for them to understand what is new or unique. If the format, content, and pedagogy were new to teachers, even the most compelling projects would not be digestible or usable for many. A familiar format paves the way for distinctive design.

Flexibility of Design to Reduce Barriers to Entry

Designers should expect that final products will represent new pedagogy and content but also make them digestible by users who are familiar with project-, problem-, or inquiry-based learning. This might require changes to the terms used to describe the various components or adapting the layout of final products such that the presentation is consistent with the users' requirements or expectations. For example, if stakeholders expect to see *essential* instead of *authentic* question, it will take nothing away from the final product to change that terminology. Or, if there are expectations around the use of instructional and project planning templates, it will not diminish the quality of the design to convert final products of this design process to use those templates. As with reducing the cognitive load on the instructor in low-priority areas (like terminology and format) in order to allocate more capacity to higher-priority areas (challenging pedagogy and content), it is helpful to anticipate and flexibly address barriers to entry in ways that do not detract from the purpose or quality of the design. When designers consider and account for potential barriers in this way, they free up their own headspace to be able to take on the challenging work ahead.

Project Components

This section describes the components of the final product. While these components will be examined more thoroughly and developed in the process outlined later in the book, this brief description can help the designer to build a mental model of the final product.

The examples in this section come from a project written in collaboration with Acero Schools Chicago. This project was selected from a set of teacher-designed projects that were intended to create culturally sustaining, C3-aligned curriculum for grades 6–8. The project was inspired by the Puerto Rican professional baseball player Roberto Clemente. In addition to being the first Latin American and Caribbean player to be inducted into the Baseball Hall of Fame, Clemente became well known for his charity efforts. The Clemente project examines the opportunity or responsibility that Black and Latinx celebrities face to advocate for their communities, and whether society rewards/punishes these efforts unevenly. The project examines this theme in historical and contemporary contexts, from a variety of perspectives.

THE AUTHENTIC QUESTION

The authentic question gives the project shape and thematic direction. This question is not easily answered and requires the user to take a position. This question is authentic to the community that is the focus of the project; its authenticity should be judged against whether or not elders, intellectuals, and scholars from within that community argue or debate it. Questions asked about a community from the perspective of an outsider would not pass such a test, nor would "devil's advocate" questions designed to provoke the reader into engagement. Ideally these questions represent a theme that has endured, that has been grappled with in multiple contexts or time periods within the community of focus. The authentic question for the Clemente project, with its associated theme and learning goal, is shown in table 2.1.

FINAL DEMONSTRATION OF KNOWLEDGE

The final demonstration of knowledge allows for students to comprehensively respond to the authentic question, demonstrating their point of view, inputs to that perspective, and understanding of counterclaims. This task should be designed to foreground the students' perspective and represent their grounding in or familiarity with the intellectual tradition of

TABLE 2.1 *Authentic question with theme and learning goal for the Clemente project*

Authentic question: Do some celebrities have more responsibility to their community than others?	
Theme	*Students will know*
Black and Latinx celebrities that advocate for their communities face scrutiny and put their careers in jeopardy. White celebrities face both less pressure to take an advocacy position and less criticism if they choose to do so.	Historical and contemporary examples of Black and Latinx celebrities engaging in advocacy and philanthropy, as well as the effects and consequences of those actions.

the community of focus. Designers consider ways that these performance tasks develop bold voices in their students, who can comprehensively and unapologetically represent their thinking, rooted in an increasing fluency with and command of their intellectual tradition. In the final product, this is typically paired with an extension to deepen students' exploration of the content. The demonstration of knowledge for the Clemente project is shown in table 2.2.

SUPPORTING QUESTIONS

Supporting questions, also known as subquestions, allow for exploring the authentic question from different vantage points, in different contexts, or from varying perspectives. Like authentic questions, supporting questions do not constitute arguments for and against what the designer believes to be right, but rather shed light on various perspectives that are authentic to the community. If one imagined elders and scholars debating a question among themselves, the supporting questions could plausibly come up. Nonmembers' questions about the community of focus would not meet this standard, though they may prepare students to anticipate and respond to counterclaims or arguments. In practice, supporting questions can emerge as part of the brainstorming of authentic questions or be added to the project map later to align with a series of tasks through which students tackle the final demonstration of knowledge for the project.

SOURCES AND FORMATIVE TASKS

These two components provide the means (sources) and opportunity (performance tasks) for students to respond to the supporting questions.

TABLE 2.2 *Final demonstration of knowledge, with extension, for the Clemente project*

Demonstration of knowledge	Extension
Construct an argument (e.g., detailed poster, outline, essay, visual presentation) in response to the compelling question, "Do Latinx celebrity/ athletes have a responsibility to their community/society?" using specific claims and relevant evidence from credible sources, while acknowledging competing views.	Create a visual depiction of some aspect of the argument (e.g., a political cartoon that expresses a student's viewpoint).

Sources can be historical document sets, with priority given to those that accurately represent the perspectives and experience of the community of focus over those written from other perspectives. Literary sources are valid here, as historical themes and truths about marginalized communities can sometimes be found more readily in literature than primary source documents. Lastly, testimonio and interviews can capture voices from students' own communities, providing an authentic and contemporary perspective.

Formative tasks allow for students to internalize and synthesize a set of findings or learnings that result from their investigations. These can be organized to examine the theme presented in the authentic question through different lenses (economic, sociopolitical, historical); to apply the same lens to multiple contexts or examples (e.g., literary or historical analysis); or to set up a schema by which students will analyze multiple cases for comparison. The example in table 2.3 illustrates how the supporting questions for the Clemente project allow for examining the theme of the unit in multiple historical contexts, applying the same lens (historical analysis) to all three. The table also shows how the supporting questions are linked to sources and formative performance tasks.

The table also shows how the supporting questions are linked to sources and formative performance tasks.

What Is Not Being Designed

The next step of the process is intended to prepare the designer to take on the challenging work ahead by eliminating constraints and adopting a design mind-set. Professional engineers and designers describe projects that are free of constraints, not following previous work, as *greenfield projects*. These projects allow the designer to start from scratch, building in any direction they like, as they might if they were building a structure in an open green field. In contrast, projects that follow previous work, impose constraints, and are organized to modify or upgrade an existing system or product are described as *brownfield projects*. Brownfield projects require designers to establish current state—known constraints—in order to incrementally improve something that already exists.

TABLE 2.3 *Supporting questions aligned with sources and formative tasks*

Supporting question 1: How can athletes/celebrities "give back" to their community or society?	
Formative performance task	*Featured sources*
Use a graphic organizer to list the ways that each athlete/celebrity "gave back" to society or community.	**Source A:** Clip about Muhammad Ali's army induction refusal **Source B:** Article about Shakira donating 10,000 pairs of shoes to citizens in her hometown **Source C:** Excerpt from Clemente biography detailing humanitarian/charitable efforts

Supporting question 2: What do athletes/celebrities risk when they speak out?	
Formative performance task	*Featured sources*
Journal entry: Who was right: Michael Jordan or Tommy Smith and John Carlos? Elaborate on your response with solid reasoning backed up by evidence from the text.	**Source A:** Article on Michael Jordan's silence, relationship to Nike and corporate interest, economic risk of speaking out **Source B:** Graph showing Jordan's Nike earnings **Source C:** Article about Tommy Smith and John Carlos, two 1968 US Olympic athletes who gave the Black Power salute on the medal stand

Supporting question 3: Is there a "right" and "wrong" way for celebrities/athletes to take a public stance on an issue?	
Formative performance task	*Featured sources*
Create a T-Chart listing three reasons why Kaepernick and others should be allowed to kneel during the national anthem. Also list three reasons why the NFL might mandate that their athletes stand and "respect" the flag. Critique the argument of the side you disagree with, supporting your argument with evidence from the text.	**Source A:** News article detailing Colin Kaepernick's refusal to stand for the national anthem prior to a preseason NFL game **Source B:** Article about Alejandro Villanueva, a Latino/Army veteran, who did not join his teammates in protest **Source C:** Article from *New York Times*: "Right and Left React to the N.F.L. Protests and Trump's Statements."

Many curriculum designers begin this work as though they were engaging in a brownfield project. We often start by assuming that current constraints, like an existing scope and sequence or our own attachment to the canon, are an accurate picture of the current state. Accepting these constraints will dramatically limit our ability to surface the most relevant and engaging themes, ideas, sources, and tasks for our students. The current state was not set up to prioritize students' community-based knowledge or cultivate them in the intellectual tradition of that community. So we begin by shunning the constraints imposed by that system. We adopt a greenfield mentality in order to surface the most compelling and authentic content. When there are materials that are compelling and transformative, designers and other stakeholders can turn their attention to digestibility. While all stakeholders' needs must be cared for, designers must care for students' needs first (introducing relevant themes, histories, and narratives that have been excluded from traditional curricula) and adult needs second (considering digestibility and adaptability of materials).

Separating Curricular Design from Instructional Decisions

It is reasonable and unsurprising that many designers begin by thinking first of their own context. Many consider not only the character and makeup of their community, but a number of local realities, even as specific as their existing curriculum's most recent scope and sequence. While many designers are writing materials for their own use, and many are used to thinking about curriculum design and instructional decisions simultaneously, it is important to pause and make a distinction between the two. Curriculum design and the choices therein relate directly and only to the curriculum, in this case the project or projects being designed. If what is being considered will not show up in the final product, it is an instructional decision, not a curriculum design choice. Instructional choices relate to how those materials will be used in a classroom. These can include decisions regarding what students will have done before and what they may do after (scope and sequence). Another example of an instructional decision is an assessment of whether students have the prior knowledge that will be necessary for the project. Yet another example might relate to perception of skill level or students with identified needs that may require additional supports or scaffolds.

It is important for this process to set aside instructional decisions. The reason is that adding constraints that can be addressed later, or that may not apply to all potential users of the final product, significantly inhibits the process of discovery. Adding constraints beyond standards or content that must be addressed immediately can be thought of as attachment to the traditional canon. If our own schooling and our current schools are rooted in the traditional canon, many of our conscious and unconscious efforts preserve that canon. Our assumptions about what must be true for a project to "fit" are references to the canon. In order to produce curriculum that leads to transformational learning experiences, designers must discern the difference between obligations (in the form of standards and mandated content) and our own attachment to the familiar.

Expressions of that attachment may sound like, "This project should focus on state history because we teach US history the following year," "My students can't even find many locations on a map, so we're going to have to start small," or "I have a lot of ELLs [English language learners], so I'll need to be thinking about text complexity from the beginning." All of these statements can be boiled down to "I can't include or address ____ because ____." Such statements ground designers in the same canonical thinking that they are, in some form or another (e.g., reading this book), seeking to disrupt. At the beginning of transformational work, it is appropriate to be critical of one's own tendencies that are grounded in a tradition that has excluded our students for decades.

All the instructional decisions just mentioned—including building prior knowledge, appropriate placement of projects in a scope and sequence, and necessary scaffolds for students with identified needs—will be accommodated. But in the meantime, designers using this process should afford themselves as much greenfield space as possible.

Various Contexts and Use Cases for Projects

Projects designed using the process outlined in this book can be used in a variety of contexts. The adaptable nature of the format and modularity of the projects lead to numerous potential implementations. Projects can be used in language arts and social studies classrooms, either to supplant a section of an otherwise traditional curriculum or as one of many projects that the teacher has selected to compose a full course. This design process invites interdisciplinary projects, referring to historical and cultural truths found in literature and in written and oral histories. It is quite reasonable to imagine that projects drawing from a variety of sources, inviting multiple potential demonstrations of student knowledge, could be used by teachers across humanities disciplines, who have expressed a desire to make their curricula more relevant to their students.[2]

In contexts where an ethnic or gender studies course is desired by the school leader, projects generated by this design process can be used to compose a full course. As discussed in the previous chapter, there is a growing demand for ethnic studies curriculum, and alignment to current pedagogy and the flexibility to enable local decision-making is key. The lack of resources aligned to current pedagogy often prevents schools from offering such courses.[3] Governing bodies are offering guidelines on the requirements for ethnic studies courses but allowing for curricular decisions to be made locally. Others struggle to articulate the content that such courses must address in order to fulfill the requirement. What is true in both contexts is that the instructional materials must reflect current thinking in social studies pedagogy, and that discussions of content center on traditional approaches to ethnic studies, with roots in the ethnic studies movements of the 1960s and 70s. The rub is twofold: current thinking regarding social studies pedagogy has not been applied to ethnic studies content, and traditional ethnic studies materials represent only four communities (Black, Chican@, Asian, and Native American), leaving out many others that seek inclusion and representation in the curriculum. The struggle over quality materials and the identities represented therein is central to the design process presented in this book: Whose histories should be explored in schools? Which narratives will be most beneficial to our students?

The answer to these questions can be visualized as a point along two axes. Along one axis is cultural relevance, along which students consistently see themselves and their elders in the histories and literature explored in the curriculum. Along this axis we might measure how frequently students interact with the intellectual tradition of their community. On the other axis is cultural richness, along which students are exposed to experiences and ideas from communities not their own. On this axis we might measure how frequently students encounter the particularity of others, grow in empathy, and learn to interpret or transfer an understanding of that particularity to their own lives.

Many of us hope for our students to have an education that is relevant first and rich second. This desire is in response to the lived reality that for many decades students of color have been offered a dramatically lopsided experience in which the burden of interpretation and transfer has been carried by students and caring teachers. Culturally sustaining opportunities for students of color have been few and far between. The poverty of culturally sustaining curricular resources is outlined clearly in seminal works on the topic of culturally relevant teaching, as well as recent analysis.[4] A primary goal of this design process is to produce a culturally sustaining curriculum in which students see themselves and their communities as the central focus. In many classrooms, the students represent a variety of communities and intellectual traditions. Where one group of students may find relevant content in a project, another group in the same classroom may find richness. Rudine Sims Bishop coined the phrase "mirrors, windows, and sliding glass doors" to describe this dynamic.[5] Different students will encounter the same project or set of projects at a different point along the two axes described earlier. Striking the right balance of relevance and richness is the work of good classroom and school leaders. The modularity of projects allows for localized decision-making such that content selections can be responsive to the needs of communities, schools, and classrooms.

When cohorts of teachers and instructional leaders have come together to produce a set of projects using this design methodology, it's been nearly impossible to accurately predict the various ways those projects would eventually be implemented. When the products are compelling and reflect the character of the student body, they find ways into the curriculum that are unique to each classroom. Some school leaders have asked that teachers implement one project in English language arts (ELA) classrooms and gain feedback from students and others before implementing more. Another school might ask teachers to organize the social studies scope and sequence such that half of the projects taught reflect students' identities. Another school might use all of the resulting projects to compose a humanities, ethnic, or gender studies elective. All of these applications of the projects would be good and wise, trusting that in each case the decision-making process balanced the needs of students to access curriculum that leads to culturally sustaining and rich learning spaces.

When designing projects, designers need not hold all potential use cases in mind, however. As noted earlier, it is better for designers to set aside instructional decisions and potential implementations (what projects, when, and so on) and instead focus their attention on designing strong projects. When designers create for themselves the mental space to make bold choices and follow a thoughtful process, they are not deprioritizing or shunning the needs of the end user. Rather, they are prioritizing the creation of a strong and compelling project. Strong and compelling projects can work and add value in a variety of contexts. Stated differently, compelling design allows for wise instructional decisions.

Adopting a Design Mind-Set

The work of ignoring perceived constraints in order to create the mental space for a greenfield project is difficult. For some it can leave the impression that their hard-earned pragmatism and habits of efficiency are wrong or problematic, which is not the case. A more productive frame might be to visualize one's established mind-set as materials and tools on a desk. If one were preparing for a challenging task that required space to work and to arrange new materials and tools, the first step might be to clear their current workspace. This is neither to criticize the materials or their utility, nor to suggest that they should be replaced. It means only that for the new project to have the best opportunity for success, the workspace must be cleared. Designers are wise to consider constraints in the same way.

While designers should set aside instructional decisions, attachment to the familiar or traditional content, and control over potential uses for final products, there are two elements they should anchor on as they prepare. First is their attachment to the students they seek to serve. If anything, it is helpful to grow in their attachment and commitment to this group of students. It may be helpful, if one finds it difficult or necessary to articulate one's conviction and commitment, to complete the following sentence: "I am committed to my _____ students because they deserve to be seen and known in my classroom/school/district."

This recommendation may seem overly dramatic, but it comes from an honest place. Designers using this process have found themselves bound up by attachments to common practice or mired in concerns of the potential impact of their efforts. In their struggle to get "unstuck," phrases such as "But my queer students deserve this—I didn't learn this in school and my students deserve better," or, "My students should be able to read authors who look like them," and "My Muslim students feel invisible" have effectively overcome these doubts. Throughout this chapter, many constraints have been set aside in service of the designer's purpose. The completion of the sentence "I am committed to my _____ students" constitutes that predominant purpose.

The other element that is helpful for the designer to anchor on is the probability that their predominant purpose is not theirs alone. If the designer, in their corner of the world, has independently come to the conclusion that their _____ students deserve to see their identity or community represented in the curriculum, others may have come to a similar conclusion. In other words, if "my students deserve better" rings true for the designer, it likely does for others as well. This raises the possibility that the designer might produce resources that will address needs beyond their immediate context. The idea that the "I" in the sentence stem might be extended to "we," and that "my _____ students" might better be said as "our _____ students," expands the designer's sights from their own context to many others. No matter the distribution plan, the notion that the designer's work is important not only to "me and mine," but to "professionals like me and students like mine," sets the stage for powerful and important work. A part of the designer's mental model of the final product should be its potential for impact. How might a designer approaching a greenfield project respond differently when the frame for their work goes from "build a good and stable structure" to "build a guidepost and inspiration for future designers"?

The next chapters present design steps that will offer opportunities to practice designing with this mind-set and form the mental habit of broadening one's frame of reference beyond the immediate context. Early design steps lend themselves to this purpose, as they are somewhat abstract. Lean in to this next step, as it will help you to make full use of all of the greenspace you have created.

II

Designing Units

CHAPTER 3

Who Will Focus My Attention?

Choosing a Focal Figure

This chapter begins the design process with an unlikely or uncommon first step: identifying a hero or protagonist from the community. This hero will introduce new themes, ideas, and people to the designer as they begin the important process of discovery. Subsequent sections will guide the designer step-by-step through that process with idea-boarding and research techniques that will surface durable historical themes. This lays the groundwork for developing the authentic question that forms the core of a culturally sustaining curriculum unit.

We Don't Yet Know What We Don't Know

To begin a curriculum design process by drawing a protagonist from the community of focus is not a common first step. Indeed, many of us have been trained to begin by determining what the learning outcomes might be, defining what evidence of learning would be sufficient, and planning backward from the endpoint. It is also common to begin with the text—a novel or historical document set that's chosen early on. For this process, we instead begin with the assumption that there is much about the community we are writing for that is unknown to us. If we are grounded in that understanding, a process of discovery and seeking to know more is a necessary first step. By taking on the role of learner-designer early, we can more easily maintain that role throughout the process.

Were we to begin by determining the texts to be studied, the desired final product, or even the standards that might be addressed, structural pieces of the unit would come together before any significant discovery had taken place. These structural pieces are constraints that future design choices must accommodate. If we ground early and significant choices in our own understanding of the community we are writing for, simply accepting that our understanding is limited, a few things are likely to happen. First, we are less likely to adopt the learner role, as we're already in decision-making mode. We have already begun to act on our own (even if significant) expertise and put our decisions down on paper. Those decisions are unlikely to be challenged or changed later on. Anything that we might learn about the community will not change these decisions; rather, it will end up as window dressing on a house that's largely been built. Another thing that will happen is that we will miss the opportunity to adopt the learner-designer role early on. This role is difficult to adopt or act on, and thus it requires practice for most of us. In taking on challenging work, we owe ourselves the best possible opportunity to take on, learn, and practice a new role.

An illustration of this dynamic might look something like this: You have a guest coming to dinner. You care greatly about this guest and want to be hospitable, and so you've chosen to prepare a dish that will make them feel right at home. You're also a very good cook; you have enough experience that you don't tend to look at recipes in advance because you already have a mental model of what you plan to make and the ingredients you'll likely need. So you start at the grocery, buying what you think will be necessary based on your intuition. Once in the kitchen, you take the time to look through recipes for the dish that you plan to make to shore up bits and pieces that you were uncertain of. You discover that some of your best guesses were not quite right. The ingredients that you chose, most of which you're comfortable and familiar with, are not authentic to the dish you've set out to make. But they are close. You choose not to return to the grocery, but rather to work with what you have. The end product and total effect is a partial success—your guest recognizes and is grateful for the effort. The dish itself is good. But because of the compromises made on the ingredients (core components), the end product is inauthentic. Your guest, consequently, does not get the flood of warm emotion one experiences with the first bite of homey, familiar food as you'd hoped.

And so we begin with the knowledge that there is much we don't yet understand, and trust that starting with discovery will serve our ultimate goal. Even so, acknowledging our own lack of understanding at the beginning of a complex, multistage process can feel unsettling, akin to looking at a 1,000-piece puzzle poured out onto a table. Most of us need a sense of the steps that we must take to be successful, and ideally their sequence, in order to begin.

Starting by identifying a protagonist, hero, or heroine from the community we're writing for serves three purposes. The first is practical, while the second and third are conceptual. The first, practical reason is that beginning with a protagonist, hero, or heroine provides a clear entry point into a complex process—like beginning with the flat-edge pieces of a puzzle. The second reason is that beginning with humans allows for an organic exploration of themes, whereas histories and literature have already undergone some synthesis. The third reason is that our students deserve curricula rooted in heroism—stories of the bold and the brilliant—to mirror the traditional canon serving the dominant group.

Starting with the Flat-Edge Pieces of the Puzzle

Most tutorials on solving a jigsaw puzzle recommend the same first step: separate out and connect the outer, flat-edge pieces first. This practice is so common that "starting with the edge pieces" has become a metaphor for applying commonsense approaches to solving complex problems. Writers on topics from workplace productivity to home organization suggest "finding the edge pieces" as the first in their recommended multistep processes. Selecting a protagonist as the first in this book's multistep process for designing a culturally sustaining curriculum serves a similar purpose: offering a clear and cogent first step that, when complete, will have created enough context that the subsequent steps are easier to follow. Separating and joining all the edge pieces of a jigsaw puzzle is easy; those pieces are easy to identify. When they are assembled, they create the frame for the finished product. In the frame, one can often see from the colors where other elements will end up—the goat will go in the upper-left corner, the rocket ship in the lower-right corner. In choosing a protagonist to research as the first step in designing curriculum, there is an equally clear starting place, as heroes and heroines can often be easily identified. In researching them, designers will be introduced to themes, characters, and events that will constitute major elements of their final products. The protagonist, like the frame of the jigsaw puzzle, may or may not be foregrounded in the final product. Indeed, this protagonist may play only a supporting role; the historical themes that are discovered in the process will be the focal point in the final product. Nonetheless, the design process benefits greatly from a first step that generates both structure and context.

The metaphor breaks down slightly in that there is only one correct way to solve a jigsaw puzzle. This is not true of designing curriculum. Some puzzle solvers, particularly younger ones, may start with a character or figure that is obvious in the lines or colors of the pieces. What they discover about this approach, however, is that it's not clear what the next step should be, or even how one major element might fit together with another. This is the purpose of the "edge pieces first" approach: sensible selection of the first step makes subsequent steps easier. This is true of the recommendation to begin with a protagonist as well. Choosing a hero as an entry point for discovery will create context, adding depth and breadth to the designer's understanding. It also prevents designers from prematurely anchoring on choices that may need to be revisited and significantly revised later. While there are a number of ways designers might organize themselves and their process to create culturally sustaining curricula, the rationale and steps described here will generate a frame for the final product and enough context to clarify subsequent steps.

Exploring Organically Versus Synthetically

Through the experience of supporting designers engaged in the process of writing curriculum intended for communities with particularity, I've had the opportunity to pressure-test a few different approaches. I would describe these as three distinct approaches, organized by the starting place of the designer. These three starting places are historical events (e.g., the 1995 Million Man March on Washington), a piece of literature (e.g., *Esperanza Rising* by Pam Muñoz Ryan), or a person (e.g., Esmeralda Santiago). What separates these three approaches is *who is doing the synthesis*. When a designer begins with a plan to write curriculum about a historical event like the Million Man March, they will typically begin with clearly defined parameters regarding what is and is not relevant. These parameters are defined by the synthesis of journalists and historians. Those journalists and historians have reviewed documents, interviewed participants, spoken with one another, and synthesized what they believe to be the most relevant information. Similarly, when a designer begins with a piece of literature, the parameters are (if anything more) clearly defined. The author has synthesized ideas, perspectives, and narratives in producing their work. Designers may review interviews or commentary relating to that work. When designers begin with a person, however, in their discovery they may encounter historical events that are not directly related. They will be introduced to other characters whose lives have intersected with their protagonist. They might anchor on writings by or about that person, the political context surrounding them at different times, their early life, or their legacy. Two designers anchoring on the same person may do radically different syntheses. This is less true when designers begin with a historical event or piece of literature. Historical events and literature are discrete, whereas human lives are expansive. Starting with a human life invites the designer into an organic exploration of themes, ideas, people, events, and artifacts. In this venue, the designer is invited to make choices and engage in the synthesis. When the starting place is a historical event or literature, the designer must react to others' syntheses.

It is also in choosing the most expansive of the three starting places that we make room for perspectives that may have been written *out* of the story as historians, journalists, and authors were doing the hard work of synthesis. As noted, the nature of synthesis is making choices about what is most relevant and what is less so. In the example of the Million Man March, it would be logical to infer that participants traveling to demonstrate relied on women in their families to fill gaps in responsibilities at home—women who were *encouraged not* to participate but were likely looked to as a support. That is not to suggest that this is right, wrong, or otherwise, but it is true that in covering the event, journalists decided that this perspective was not important enough to include in their coverage. Would a curriculum designer, researching the life of an organizer of that event, come to the same conclusion? In *Esperanza Rising*, Pam Muñoz Ryan focuses on themes of class and migration. The full historical context of the setting is not thoroughly explored—and rightly so. The author made choices regarding what would support the story and what would distract from it. She does not examine US immigration policy in the 1920s and 1930s, but a curriculum designer researching the author—who was born in Bakersfield, California, in the 1950s and went on to write many notable books exploring social themes around Mexican American identity—might.

This phase of the design process invites the designer to engage in discovery in an organic fashion. They will begin to tease out connections between people, events, artifacts, politics, and time. In the subsequent design phase, the designer will begin to synthesize these connections by developing questions. Selecting histories, literature, and narratives to allow for the exploration of these questions will follow. By choosing the most expansive of the three starting places, designers give themselves more room to engage in discovery and meaning-making.

Telling the Stories of the Bright and Bold

The third reason to begin designing curriculum by surfacing heroes, heroines, or protagonists is that students deserve to know bold and brilliant characters that come from similar communities, in order to mirror the traditional canon serving the dominant group. The traditional canon has overrepresented White and European characters in US schooling, an imbalance bolstered by overrepresentation in other social venues and media. The result is a deep and shared familiarity with White (predominantly male) characters across all demographics. Whether you are White, Black, Native, Filipino, queer, or Latinx, you are expected to be familiar with a large cast of White, mostly male heroes.

Picture a dinner-party or watercooler conversation with a set of friends or colleagues that includes people of different ethnicities, genders, and generations. One member of the group references Mozart, George Washington, JFK, or Bill Gates. The reference does not include any explanation or context for who that person is; there is a baseline expectation of familiarity. Imagine the looks of disbelief if any participant in that conversation were to pause and ask, "Who is JFK?" There would be real social costs for unfamiliarity with any of these names.

The cast of characters is also substantial. It includes figures from the arts, sciences, business, and politics spanning many generations. I would imagine there are hundreds of names that could be used in place of the four examples just given. There is, in the traditional canon, sufficient reinforcement for the prominence of Whiteness to suggest that the same dinner-party or watercooler conversation would play out similarly with a broad cast of characters from many time periods and sectors.

Now picture the same scenario where a friend or colleague references Sor Juana Inés de la Cruz, Benito Juarez, Guillermo González Camarena, or Felipe Calderón. There would be an expectation of an explanation of who they are and commentary on their context. To not include additional information might irritate the other participants. These are noncanonical characters, and so their presence in the conversation needs to be justified and explained. What would it mean for our students to add to and create a new canon of characters that do not require explanation or justification?

There are people of color included in the traditional canon. One might argue that if Rev. Dr. Martin Luther King Jr., Cesar Chavez, or Harvey Milk were referenced during a dinner-party or watercooler conversation, they would not require introduction either. This is true, and also surfaces a separate important truth about canonical characters, particularly in the curriculum. As mentioned in the previous chapter, what one might know about Black history based on information presented in an average US history textbook amounts to cursory information about a handful of major events between the 1600s and today, and introduction to a small number of civil rights heroes and heroines spanning the same time period.[1] It is notable that all of the examples provided are situated in a struggle with oppression. These stories are important, and worthy of exploration and study in our classrooms. It is also true that if the goal of this design work is equity, our students are owed a broader cast of characters, representing a fuller representation of the life of the community. Are there not poets, architects, innovators, and businesspeople to be discussed? To reproduce the benefits of familiarity for all of our students, we must access a similarly diverse range of experiences. Do students belonging to dominant groups primarily study struggle and oppression?

To understand the effects of centering struggle, oppression, and injustice, we can look to Holocaust education and what was gained when efforts shifted from a focus on tragedy to heroes, heroines, and protagonists. Much of Holocaust education was organized around events, facts, and statistics. This is no fault of the educators engaged in this work, as this was during an era in which history education was organized much the same way. Those events, facts, and statistics were also horrific in nature, but important learning so as to prevent the minimization and erasure of this history so many rightly feared. This approach also exacerbated the transmission of generational trauma and grief to the children and grandchildren of Holocaust survivors. In an effort to shift this dynamic, Holocaust educators refocused efforts on the testimonies of survivors—recognizing them as exceptions—and the stories of rescuers and resistors. While the facts, events, and statistics were consistent in the two approaches, the focus on individuals' stories of heroism contributed to the psychological health of the students.[2]

While this example is situated in a struggle with oppression, we can tease out the effects of centering on heroines and protagonists. When learning objectives were designed around facing the terrible and grim realities of oppression, students reflected back an experience of demoralization. When learning objectives were instead designed around humanizing the experience of survival and resistance, students demonstrated an increased sense of agency and resilience. How might this dynamic play out when designing curriculum that introduces students to a broad range of protagonists representing roles and contributions beyond resistors and advocates?

How to Look and What to Look For

Some of us are lucky enough to live in cities that have named streets and schools after heroes or heroines from the communities we write for. I personally have worked in schools that were named for authors, artists, politicians, and philanthropists from the community that the schools served. In many of these cases, however, the students and staff were unfamiliar with the accomplishments, lives, and legacies of these people. Researching these people produced ample material for discussion, generated ideas to be explored, and introduced new figures for further discovery. Those people that communities have named schools (and other important institutions) after are frequently both prominent enough that writings by and about them are not difficult to find and obscure enough that designers will generate new and valuable learning.

Many designers do not live or work in places with schools named after historical figures representing the community they are writing for. Another entry point can be brief *articles-as-lists* on a role or identity within the community. Writers, journalists, and experts have compiled information in this way in the digital space for decades, and the article-as-list has been a popular journalistic format since the nineteenth century. Pragmatically, searches for "prominent Vietnamese artists," "prominent Black businesswomen," and "prominent LGBT politicians" will all produce lists of people, including a brief introduction or synopsis of their contributions. Some articles-as-lists will not qualify as expert-curated resources, and taking the time to find one from a reliable source is recommended. In any case, this method meets the goal of gaining an introduction to a protagonist.

Teasing Out a Theme: Idea-Boarding

When a protagonist has been identified, the initial discovery phase should generate multiple entry points for the designer into that person's life and story. These entry points can be thought of as ideas posted on a board rather than points on a story line. They need not be connected. They should not be organized linearly. These entry points are like seeds that will sprout shoots, that will become roots and grow together.

Begin by searching out quotes and then parsing out the context for the quote. This can lead to interviews, speeches, or writings by the figure. In the spirit of prioritizing the organic over the synthesized, searching for quotes allows the designer to begin with the least synthesized material possible. When you've generated a few quotes of interest, note whether they came from writings, an interview, or a speech, and then try to find the full text or transcript. While reading the full text, note themes and ideas.

Make note of references to people or events that you're unfamiliar with. Think of these references to others as an introduction. People introduced in this way may be equally or more interesting for research. They may help to uncover an historical truth, line of thinking, or set of events that could become a through line in the design. Cultivate the offshoots that are the most interesting.

Also make note of phrases that are particularly resonant. Others may have used this quote in subsequent years to connect the protagonist's work to their own. This will allow the designer to tease out a historical theme. When a protagonist is quoted by another in a different context and time period, there is potential to uncover important connections. These connections between protagonists, heroes, and heroines within a community are profound and valuable. They could be thought of as a root system that is complex and hidden from view. A deep understanding of that system of connection—how people's work and ideas connect with others in different time periods and contexts, how one's work builds upon another's, how the protagonists differ, and so on—is the hallmark of an expert, elder, or scholar. The approach of using quotes to connect a protagonist to others' work is equivalent to noticing the same species of plants in an environment and guessing at their connection, imagining what the root structure might look like. The notion of guessing at or imagining what connections exist or how they were made may not sound appealing or satisfying; however, beginning to understand the connections between heroes and heroines within a community across time is powerful. Discovering a quote, understanding its origin, and finding instances of others referring to it suggests an enduring theme. Durable historical themes are important structural elements for curriculum designers.

The next step is to research the historical context for the quote. Note the time period and what events and political or social realities the protagonist may have been reacting to. What decisions were being made that would affect the protagonist's community? Were they reacting to decisions, trying to influence them? The *grain size*, or level of detail, for this information need not be too small or specific. This type of information can be found in commentary on the quote itself. Note the events, decisions, and social or political realities in commentary and then research them separately in order to develop a broad understanding. This step serves to better ground the designer's understanding of the protagonist's motivations, which in turn allows the designer to better steer clear of misconceptions—particularly important when writing for a community that is unfamiliar. The possibility for misinterpretation and misconception in this process is enormous, even when the designer identifies with the community being written for. Developing some familiarity with the goings on around a given quote will build important background knowledge for the designer and mitigate the possibility of misconception.

In the next step in the idea-boarding process, we continue this trajectory from the most organic sources (quotes from interviews, speeches, writing) to more synthesized ones. We now work to place the quote in the context of the person's life and work using biographical resources. This will add depth to the designer's understanding of the protagonist's motivations. What happened before this speech or interview, and what happened after? What was this person reacting to in their own life experience? What might be learned about their background that would offer perspective on their value system? How did the attitudes, ideas, and perspective captured in one moment in time (the interview, speech, or writing the quote was drawn from and the social reality surrounding the protagonist at that time) carry forward? What were their next actions? Who did they influence to move the work forward? Answers to these questions will allow the designer to add breadth to their understanding of the protagonist's life and work. It will also add depth to the emerging historical theme that the designer is discovering to guide the evolution of the project.

Examples from the Design Cohort
Cam

Cam set out to write a project for grades 4 and 5 about LGBT-headed families. Through looking for heroes or heroines specific to that area of community life, Cam was able to surface a quote from Bill Jones, an advocate for family and parental rights for LGBT people, in the interview references to court cases and civil actions specific to LGBT family issues.

The interview also included advice on parenting, communities of support, and a number of other topics relevant to gay parents.

In looking up some of the court cases and civil actions mentioned in the interview, Cam discovered research specific to LGBT family advocacy. He found that there was in fact a large body of research on instances of LGBT-headed families advocating for changes that would directly impact their families but also resulted in lasting cumulative impacts on LGBT rights writ large. Cam's articulation of the theme that was emerging from case law and related research was, "There is a separate stream of research on this parallel movement of normal, everyday people changing laws case by case that fueled the larger and more visible LGBT rights movement. Dads winning custody battles and lesbians adopting kids laid the legal foundation for all kinds of rights issues, but the people who won them are less visible because following those victories they went back to living their lives."

Cam's research began to coalesce around the theme of families advocating for the legal changes they needed in order to live, and the ways that very personal struggle for rights supported and fueled a more visible set of advocacy strategies.

Malika

Malika began her research with a historic figure: King Ashama, a seventh-century emperor of Axum, a region that now includes Eritrea and parts of surrounding nations. She describes King Ashama as a benevolent and well-loved figure in Eritrean history. King Ashama was known in part for having welcomed refugees from a warring neighbor even given religious and ethnic differences. Malika reflected that Eritreans take pride in this narrative and that being a welcoming nation, even across religious and ethnic differences, is likewise a point of pride.

Further research uncovered a number of ways that historians believe that King Ashama's actions benefited the nation. The general goodwill that King Ashama demonstrated made him an influential figure in the region, a fact which served Eritrea in a variety of ways. Welcoming refugees seemed to have opened relationships with neighboring nations that enabled trade. Political alliances also made Eritrea safe and strong militarily. These benefits to Eritrea's health and strength speak to Ashama's wisdom in addition to his benevolent character.

This line of research surfaced conflict between values that Eritreans hold regarding the treatment of refugees and the reception many Eritreans received as refugees and immigrants themselves. King Ashama represents the widely held Eritrean cultural value of inclusion and protection of vulnerable people. Eritreans received varying degrees of inclusion and protection as immigrants, which highlights the relationship between a nation's treatment of refugees and the character of its leaders.

David

David sought to write a project to explore the ways that social injustices can compound and accumulate. The idea that the oppression of past generations can influence one's worldview and outlook is not often discussed openly with students. These accumulated injustices can have a significant social cost. This theme was of particular interest given his perspective on the political environment in 2020 under the Trump administration, and the costs of the politics of fear, which disproportionately affect marginalized communities.

David's intention was to focus on marginalization broadly for a high school unit. The prompt to highlight the stories of the bright and bold by starting with a protagonist surfaced quotes from artist Kendrick Lamar. The first hip hop artist to win the Pulitzer Prize, Lamar explores the relationship between intergenerational trauma and accumulated fear in both his interviews and his lyrics. Quotes and articles connected Lamar to contemporary figures grappling with similar themes, including author Ta-Nehisi Coates and others.

In interviews and excerpts, Lamar and Coates address both the lived reality of accumulated fear and also potential responses. Beyond the existence of accumulated fears and the role of intergenerational trauma in the Black community, David's research suggested that the artists and authors he was reading believed that art had a special role to play in helping communities to process these traumas. A theme of both recognition and a desire to respond to fear and trauma began to emerge.

Annabeth

Annabeth set out to write a project for middle schoolers about underrepresented people's history in colonial America. She, at the outset, considered surfacing women's history, Black history, and the histories of native peoples. For her discovery process she began with John Punch, a Black American who, when fleeing indentured servitude alongside two White peers, was sentenced to a lifetime of slavery. His two White peers were sentenced to extended servitude. Punch is thought to be among the first Americans to be sentenced to slavery, constituting an important, even pivotal, moment in US history—the advent of slavery.

Quotes from Punch and other Black contemporaries were difficult for Annabeth to uncover. Punch also did not meet the criteria to be considered a protagonist as defined by other designers. It is true that the decision to focus on John Punch introduced themes around struggle with oppression, perhaps the most prominent example in US history. Nonetheless, Annabeth continued in her discovery, exploring implications for the court's decision and reactions from historians and writers.

In reading Black historians' commentary on the colonial period, Annabeth found that the clear and consistent theme was that dominant historical accounts of this period in US history underrepresent the resistance of enslaved peoples. These historians suggest that the untold stories and hidden histories—were they unearthed, discussed, and understood—would change our understanding of the society we live in now.

CHAPTER 4

What Is My Authentic Question?

This chapter takes the emergent historical themes that were identified in the previous chapter and uses them to craft *authentic questions*— that is, questions that are authentic to the community of focus and form the spine of the project. A critical step in formulating authentic questions is connecting with an elder, scholar, or expert who is deeply familiar with the intellectual tradition of the community of focus.

How Are Authentic Questions Different, and Why Does It Matter?

It is important to begin this phase acknowledging that most curriculum designers are practiced and comfortable composing questions to frame units. There is a large body of literature on using essential questions to frame units of study in a way that will be engaging for students. This practice in curriculum and unit writing is common enough to the field that most teacher preparation programs guide the development of the practice, and it is a common component of teachers' instructional planning. Some elements of essential questions agreed upon by both researchers and practitioners are that they are timeless, elemental, and vital for student understanding.[1]

The writers of the C3 (College, Career, and Civic Life) Framework for Social Studies State Standards developed an approach for planning social studies inquiries called the Inquiry Design Model (IDM).[2] The IDM uses a compelling question to frame an inquiry. The compelling question is explored through supporting questions, which often are more specific but related to the overarching compelling question. For questions to be compelling, they need to be both intellectually meaty and explorable through multiple disciplines, according to the IDM authors. This means that for a question to be compelling it must be relevant to at least a subset, if not all, of the social science disciplines (economics, geography, civics, history).

There are still more frameworks that guide the development of questions. Next Generation Science Standards ask students to respond to questions about the natural and designed world and the way that it works. The Common Core State Standards for math position students to ask questions like mathematicians via the standards for mathematical practice. Those teaching multiple subjects bear the burden of straddling different disciplines' notions of the nature of questions. Balancing these differences, as well as the need for specificity in creating usable instructional plans, makes this design practice difficult.

My reason for calling out this range of experience and breadth of thinking on the development of questions is to foreground for designers the ideas, preferences, and assumptions that we bring into this phase of the design process. There are many schools of thought, applied approaches, and discipline-specific ideas associated with developing questions. What is still absent from the body of work around questioning, however, is the concept of developing questions with authenticity to a non-White intellectual tradition.

Previous chapters introduced the notion that our students belong to an intellectual tradition, or that an intellectual tradition exists that intersects with their identities, as well as the fact that there is a dominant intellectual tradition that is overrepresented in US schooling and curriculum. This overrepresentation colors designers' thinking and informs our choices. This is certainly evident in how we write questions. Would one's intellectual tradition not inform what we consider to be essential, intellectually meaty, or vital for student learning?

To approach this idea from a different angle, we can begin with the ways our brains make meaning out of the information they take in. When we encounter a new piece of information, the brain looks for something it already knows that is similar. If the brain can find that similar thing to attach the new information to, and goes through the exercise of *doing something new* with that information, then it turns the new information into knowledge. The new information is stored differently and, if practiced regularly, even physically changes the brain by creating new pathways for information to travel. If these criteria are not met, the brain might store the new information for a short time but will not retain it long-term.

This logic chain suggests that the information we encounter and patterns our brains practice on a daily basis do not equally predispose us to all learning. The information we interact with and cognitive tasks we regularly engage in change our minds over time. Stated differently, the lives we lead change our brains and the way we think. When applied to instructional and learning design, the relevant principle is that *all learning is culturally mediated*. When I hear a lecture or read an article, I do not stop being the person I am or thinking the way I do, which is informed by my experiences, preferences, and practices. I cannot remove my cultural lenses in a learning experience. When I encounter a new learning that resonates with me—that I can connect with personally or presents an idea in a way that is similar to how my brain has made sense or meaning in the past—I am dramatically more likely to engage with and retain that information.

This begs the question: Would people from a community, whose lives are dramatically different because of a shared set of experiences, ask the same questions as people from the dominant group? Might a second-generation high school student have dramatically different questions about justice and fairness in a civics class? In preparing unit and lesson plans, would a Black, female teacher read *Hidden Figures* and draw different conclusions about the essential themes than her White male colleague? Might a gender-fluid person who has consciously struggled with themes of safety and belonging for many of their waking hours, for much of their life, find the same questions compelling as their cisgendered counterparts?

What this line of thinking suggests for this design process is that when we center the histories, narratives, and stories of a community with particularity, our questions must be authentic to that community. It would be a misstep to take time and care in adopting a posture of learner-designer only to allow inertia to take over the question-writing process. Equal care must be applied to the process of developing questions. The goal of this chapter is to equip the designer with the disposition, resources, and ordered steps necessary to write questions that will be authentic to the community being written for.

Phone a Friend: Connecting with Elders and Scholars

It is not possible, in a short period of time, to come to a deep knowing of an intellectual tradition that is not your own. The deep knowing referenced here requires a comfort with a broad range of expressions of that tradition. These expressions might include poetry, scholarship, civic history, and fine arts. Deep knowing also requires familiarity with the tradition across the dimension of time. Traditions evolve and are shaped along timelines measured in generations. For one to fully understand a current expression of a given tradition, one should be able to describe the roots of that expression, who and what influenced the expression, and what the evolutionary path might look like. What this deep knowing produces is *fluency*. When a person can discuss a tradition and reference multiple expressions, describe the relationships between them, and trace their evolution over generations fluidly, they demonstrate deep knowing.

No two designers come to this work with the same level of familiarity with the intellectual tradition of the community they're writing for. Some designers have more exposure or knowledge of the intellectual tradition of the community being written for than others. Some identify personally as part of that community, or there are aspects of community life that intersect with their identity. This can produce enough familiarity that the designer has good instincts, and even potentially partial fluency. This is not to suggest that designers who do not identify with the community of focus and those who come from that community themselves are starting from the same place. When a designer personally identifies as a member of the community they're writing for, their life experiences and background knowledge inform their choices in positive ways. What is still true, however, is that the depth and breadth of exposure required for fluency has typically not been offered to them. Few have been availed of the necessary breadth of exposure, sustained over time, to develop fluency. For both designers that are writing for their own community and those with more personal distance, connection to an elder or scholar is a benefit.

Elders and scholars have developed deep knowledge of an intellectual tradition. That development is often formalized by a degree and a position. Many colleges and universities have departments dedicated to ethnic and gender studies, and others have faculty with relevant research interests or backgrounds described in their online bios. It is worthwhile to seek out scholars who have accumulated knowledge and understanding related to the community being written for.

Sometimes having deep knowledge of a community's intellectual tradition is not formalized by a degree or position. Some intellectual traditions have yet to be embraced and codified by higher education. Indeed, the fields of ethnic and gender studies are relatively new to the academy, having gained critical mass in the 1960s. In some cases, community elders will have the greatest knowledge and fluency. The depth and breadth of knowledge that fuels their fluency has been gained by immersion in and years of service to a community. These elders may lead or serve community nonprofit organizations or advocacy groups and can be discovered through those associations. They may have written or given talks on topics relevant to their community and could be identified through publication.

For both scholars and elders, two things tend to be true. The first is that they are so dedicated to their community of focus that they are glad participants in any worthwhile educational effort will raise awareness for that community. The second is that they have so much information at their disposal that they are grateful for the direction and focus provided by designers. For these two reasons, when reaching out to scholars and elders, designers should provide sufficient information to paint a clear picture of what is being designed, who will use it, and why. Using previous experiences to anticipate the questions that will likely come up, I have crafted communications for designers to use in reaching out to scholars and elders, an example of which is shown in box 4.1.

BOX 4.1 *Sample letter to an expert in an intellectual tradition*

Hello EXPERT/SCHOLAR'S NAME,

My name is YOUR NAME. I'm a YOUR ROLE at YOUR SCHOOL/ ORGANIZATION. This spring I'm participating in a curriculum design cohort. We're working together on curriculum that centers on histories, literature, and narratives that are underrepresented in traditional curricula.

The design cohort is being hosted by YOUR DISTRICT OR ORGANIZA- TION. We serve NUMBER OF SCHOOLS OR STUDENTS. This cohort is also in collaboration with BRIEF DESCRIPTION OF ANY PARTNER ORGANIZATIONS. In addition to our own contexts, we plan to make all the resources that we produce freely available to the larger community.

I plan to write a project addressing YOUR TOPIC IN 8–10 WORDS. A re- quirement of the cohort is to connect with a scholar who has relevant expertise and might serve as a sounding board in the design process. In most cases, this involves two or three phone conversations and two requests for feedback on specific components of the project between ROUGH TIMELINE. For the curriculum to fully honor the community that I'm focused on, I will need sup- port from people with deep expertise. Knowledge of pedagogy and curriculum design is helpful but not required—your deep knowledge of COMMUNITY YOUR PROJECT IS FOCUSED ON would contribute much.

My thanks in advance for your consideration of my request. You can direct any questions that you have about this program to PARTNER ORGANIZA- TION'S GENERAL CONTACT and any questions that you have for me to YOUR EMAIL.

       All my best,

       YOUR NAME AND PREFERRED SALUTATION

It might seem comical or controlling to provide such a letter to de- signers. However, the relationship between the designer and the elder or scholar is pivotal for this process. Designers can be reticent, and elders or scholars require a good deal of context to maximize their impact. Many designers' tendency is to approach scholars in a way that is intended to honor their expertise and to take a posture of deference. This does not of- fer their partner enough information and context to be a good contributor. Designers have built up a depth and breadth of knowledge on instructional design, current educational practices, and curriculum that the elder or scholar must rely on. The example in box 4.1 and similar communications in subsequent steps set up the right dynamics for a fruitful collaboration. The designer owns the process—that is, sketches and prototypes components of the end product. The elder or scholar offers feedback on specific components, checking for authenticity and fluency.

Writing Authentic Questions: What Question Does the Protagonist's Life Beg?

In this step designers look back on the idea board that was created in the previous step. We will use the quotes, people, and events we discovered in that process to generate tentative questions that we believe are surfacing an enduring theme in a way that is authentic to the community we are writing for.

Choosing to use our heroine, hero, or protagonist's perspective to compose draft questions serves two purposes. The first is that it acknowledges our own *positionality* as questioners—that is, the ways in which our own race, gender, ethnicity, and class status color our worldview and thus impact the questions we ask. For this step, we attempt to look at the world through the eyes of our protagonist. This is more than, and not quite, an empathy-building exercise. Knowing some things about the protagonist's life, context, and accomplishments, we wonder, *What would they ask of their community or society today?* This is far from a perfect process and should not be expected to mitigate our positionality as questioners or designers. Even fully recognizing positionality, it should produce questions that do two things.

First, these questions should center the experience of the protagonist in their context and community. We hope to identify *their question*, and ideally in a way that is relevant to their community. We don't seek to ask questions about them or their experience amounting to some version of, "What would it have been like to be them?" We seek to situate the authentic question, and all the design decisions that will flow from it, within and from the perspective of that community.

The second thing these draft questions should do is connect our protagonist's life to our students' lived experience. The frame for this step— *what question does your hero's life beg?*—is intended to surface a theme that is identifiable, clear, or even loud in their story and relevant today. If we're able to articulate a question that is clear and present in the story of the protagonist and also relevant today, we have a promising lead on a durable historical theme.

In future steps, the durable historical theme will be presented in different contexts and time periods. It will be examined from different perspectives and "pressure-tested" such that it is engaged rigorously. The theme will be explored in past contexts and in society today.

To compose questions, it is recommended that designers return to a quote or quotes from their protagonist. If this quote was readily findable, chances are that others believe it speaks to a noteworthy theme of this person's life. The designer should then review their notes on the context. Review the social and political reality at that time, and life experiences that informed the person's perspective, as well as what came after. Reflect on the following questions:

- *Does this quote point me to a theme that is bright and bold?*
- *With the benefit of hindsight (knowing what happened next), how might I articulate the theme?*
- *Does this theme give me enough to go on? Is it substantive enough to capture my attention?*

If the answer to more than one of these questions is no or maybe, it is recommended that the designer return to the idea-boarding step. It can be challenging to tease out a durable historical theme, but it is immensely important. When the theme is clear, all subsequent design choices become easier.

If the answer to these questions is yes or mostly, the designer can begin to compose questions. Designers should aim to write three or four questions centering on the theme, through the lens of their protagonist, that can be shared and discussed with a scholar of their choosing.

The questions must also hold tension. If a question holds tension, it is not easily answered and could be justifiably answered in a variety of ways. These questions should be written such that they could lead to contradictory or opposing conclusions. If the questions we ask lack tension—if they suggest the correct conclusion—the unit we create or the instructional time we spend with students will be just an extended point-making exercise. It would be more efficient for all parties to tell students what we think, assure them of our correctness, and move on.

The nature of the tension, potentially contradictory or opposing conclusions, should be rooted in an understanding of authenticity to the community of focus. A "devil's advocate" version of this tension would not be authentic to a discussion among scholars and elders within the community. When designing curriculum for marginalized communities, examine any potentially problematic questions through this lens: Would members of the community pose that question about themselves or their experiences? If a designer is concerned about the articulation of their question and whether or not it may open up problematic discourse, it is recommended that they interrogate the authenticity of the question.

Examples from the Design Cohort

Cam

Cam's research on LGBT-headed families surfaced a theme of families advocating for changes that would directly affect them, often in response to inequities enforced by current laws or regulations. In many cases this took the shape of LGBT-headed families not being recognized as such or offered the full rights and privileges afforded to other families. Cam's research of heroes and heroines who had engaged in these battles for inclusion begged the question, "What makes a family?"

However, Cam and fellow designers grappled with whether this articulation of the question was suitable for fourth- and fifth-grade students. It would be problematic if it allowed for students to argue that only heterosexual unions (marriages) make families. Cam suggested that this question should be posed such that the discourse would be "held in the light" and avoid arguments that would be damaging to LGBT students and teachers. It would be problematic to write a project that asked students to argue for or against the legitimacy of LGBT-headed families. It would also be entirely inauthentic to the LGBT community. The litmus test for authenticity is whether or not those deeply familiar with the intellectual tradition of their community would find a question worthy of discussion.

Cam came to an articulation of this theme that both held the discourse in the light and was authentic to the LGBT community: "How have families changed history?" Cam was able to connect with Michael Bronski, author of *A Queer History of the United States* (Beacon Press, 2011) and a professor of practice in media and activism in the Women, Gender, and Sexuality program at Harvard University. Bronski reasoned that the term *families* may be narrowly focused on those with children, noting that many LGBTQ people do not have children or may create their own chosen families. While the idea of people fighting for equality through family case law is compelling, it is at odds with this important dynamic in the LGBTQ community. Bronski suggested that the same theme could be more authentically addressed by a question that juxtaposes legal and social equality, such as "What is more important, legal equality or social equality?" A question like this would allow for students to examine the relationship between cases fought for equality and evidence of social equality, such as opinion polls, representation in media, and representation in leadership. Bronski noted that this question is authentic both to the LGBTQ movement and to the intellectual tradition of studying LGBTQ history.

Malika

Malika's discovery coalesced around the theme of inclusion and welcoming of immigrants as an Eritrean cultural value, exemplified by historical leaders. The idea that leaders' wisdom and character could be assessed through their treatment of immigrants was prominent in both historical and contemporary contexts. Many leaders within the Eritrean diaspora argue for better treatment of immigrants on the grounds of future benefits and social values. An early draft of a question that would allow for exploration of this theme both in historical and contemporary contexts was "Does a nation put its power at risk when welcoming immigrants?"

Malika's concern with this articulation of the question was that it did not center on the role of leaders, their wisdom, and their values. She imagined a project in which students could analyze leaders' wisdom and character through their treatment of immigrants, first in historical Eritrea and later through experiences of the Eritrean diaspora, both as immigrants themselves and later as leaders advocating for inclusion. The notion that students could apply this analysis to leaders in different contexts, and also be introduced to many benevolent Eritrean leaders, was compelling.

A question that got at this theme in a way that would be authentic to Malika's emerging vision for the project was "What does a nation's treatment of immigrants say about its leaders?" Malika was able to connect with Dr. Michael Ralph, director of the Africana Studies Department at New York University, who agreed to consult with her over the course of her design work. Dr. Ralph encouraged Malika to include examples of Eritrean leaders in the US that students would connect with to serve the relevance of the project. Ultimately, her authentic question became "What does the way a nation treats immigrants say about its leaders?"

David

David researched the events that lead or flow into marginalization and the lasting effects it has. David had discussions with Shantá R. Robinson, an assistant professor in the University of Chicago's School of Social Service Administration. First, these discussions clarified the need to accurately identify and develop a working definition of marginalization as a prerequisite for the project. Second, Dr. Robinson suggested a deeper look into ways generational trauma can be passed down through the physical body and the science behind this phenomenon. One of David's original questions—"Can a community accumulate fear, and what are the impacts?"—was reframed as "Where is accumulated fear kept, and how does it manifest in our communities?" This rearticulation of the question, by driving at the physicality of accumulated fear and generational trauma as Dr. Robinson recommended, is more authentic to the Black and Latinx intellectual traditions.

In response to David's question, "How can communities process generational fear and trauma?" Robinson suggested that responses relevant to this project would fall into two categories of action: social justice movements and writing the real story. The former points to the work of activists responding to ongoing causes of trauma by organizing. The latter is an empowerment of Black communities to analyze their existence without the White gaze, to celebrate the existence of the community rather than ponder past fears, and to tell the real story from the perspective of communities that experienced the generational fear or trauma.

This discussion led to a new articulation of the authentic question for the project, focused by the direction of Dr. Robinson: "How can communities respond to generational trauma?"

Annabeth

Annabeth was able to have meaningful conversations with two scholars: Dr. Yohuru Williams, the dean of the College of Arts and Sciences at the University of St. Thomas, and Dr. Benjamin Fitzpatrick, a professor of humanities and social sciences at Morehead State University. Having identified a broad topic of slavery, Annabeth struggled to find an angle that would be narrow enough to articulate a clear, authentic question. Discussions of various potential narratives and interpretations of laws with Dr. Williams and Dr. Fitzpatrick gave rise to the idea of reparations as a focus. Dr. Fitzpatrick suggested that this topic was debatable and relevant to policy makers and historians alike.

Annabeth wanted to articulate a question that would encourage discussion not of the legitimacy of reparations, but rather of the history and various perspectives on the modern controversy. She considered questions such as "Are reparations feasible today?", "Are reparations necessary for healing?" and "Is 'sorry' enough?" ultimately deciding to move forward with "Why are reparations controversial?"

CHAPTER 5

What Will Students Know
and Be Able to Do?

The previous chapter illustrated how designers can seek support from an elder or scholar with deep knowledge of the intellectual tradition of the community being written for. This relationship is meant to share perspectives on the authenticity of the questions that the project will be organized to answer. Designers draft questions from the vantage point of their protagonist in order to situate their questions within the community of focus, while making connections to students' lived experiences. This chapter will explore students' relationship to content, examining what content has what effects such that designers can make thoughtful choices about what will best support the desired learning experience. Determining the content on which their projects will center equips designers to write a final demonstration of knowledge and select sources in subsequent steps.

Content Knowledge: What Matters and Why?

There are a number of arguments for better and more diverse representation in the curriculum. For designers, these arguments have become beliefs that motivate them to engage in this work. Examples might include: "It is wrong for students to not see themselves in the curriculum because erasure is an expression of systemic racism," "There are social-emotional benefits when students do see themselves in the curriculum," and "Students deserve to know their own history." These are important and compelling beliefs, but they are often offset by simultaneous beliefs such as, "There are things all students simply need to know in order to be successful," "My students don't have important background knowledge because the system has failed them," or "Changes to the curriculum will create knowledge gaps that will hurt students in the future." As with the first set of beliefs, these beliefs are arrived at honestly—there are arguments behind them that are supported by research and reinforced by many educators' experience. It is important to examine both beliefs that are aligned with the design process and those that are potential barriers, and to anchor on the former category. This is not to say that misaligned beliefs are invalid, but rather that they will disrupt the design process if not set aside.

The Privileging Effects of Familiarity

The arguments that will serve as drivers for this design process are: "Students have background knowledge and leveraging that serves more rigorous skill development," "Students are owed a knowledge of their own history and of those like them," "Representation serves students' development of a healthy self-concept," and "There is nothing specifically beneficial about the traditional canon." The umbrella term I use to call these arguments to mind, introduced in chapter 1, is *the privileging effect of familiarity*. The reasoning behind the term is that it does not benefit designers to anchor on beliefs regarding what is wrong with the status quo; righting a wrong or addressing a deficit is less clear, directionally, than reproducing a success. The *privileging effect of familiarity* refers to the benefits that students in the dominant group get within the current system. Students are benefited by seeing people who look like them in literature and history, engaging in discourse around shared or common experiences, and being exposed to themes and ideas they can discuss with their parents and caregivers. These features of the curriculum privilege the knowledge, identity, and resources of some students over others. When these features and benefits are understood, designers can use them to privilege their own students' knowledge, identity, and resources.

Understanding a feature and its benefits is a tool that a designer can use—and a tool is more useful to a designer than a position. This section will unpack these arguments in order to equip the designer with tools to make choices that will serve their projects, and ultimately their students.

Students Have Background Knowledge

Human beings gain information and build knowledge in the course of daily life, through their educational pursuits, experiences, and interactions with peers and elders. Students from all backgrounds and communities are presented with ideas and offered opportunities to test and use them, reinforcing and adding to their existing knowledge. If there were a uniform measure that could assess everyone's knowledge, certainly we would find that knowledge is not perfectly and evenly distributed among all people walking the earth. It is valuable to call out, however, that those involved with schooling have a terribly confused notion of knowledge, specifically what is useful and what is not.

In K–12 education, the term *background knowledge* (or *prior knowledge*) tends to refer to "what students know and learned before they came into the classroom or school." This working definition does not distinguish between what students know from their lives and what they learned in their previous history or science class. Scholarly works tend not to distinguish between sources of knowledge in these discussions, either.[1] Background knowledge is often defined by the educator's assessment of the absence or lack of it. The educator might diagnose a deficit of knowledge after noticing a student's inability to access a text, engage with a topic, or invest themselves in a set of learning experiences. There are some assessments of prior knowledge that are more defined, such as vocabulary assessments before a unit of study, designed to equip students with the necessary lexicon early on. Not all discussions of background knowledge, assessments, or efforts to build necessary knowledge are this disciplined. As with many discussions meant to define and diagnose a deficit, students of color and low-income White students tend to be problematized in our daily conversations around background knowledge. It is reasonable to question, however, whether the very same assessment used to problematize students' knowledge could instead be a reflection of the learning experiences, texts, and topics. If we define lack of relevant background knowledge only in relation to a fixed set of learnings that we've established, concluding that the fixed set of learnings is a mismatch is far more reasonable than the highly problematic conclusion that "my students just don't know things." If we assume that human beings have knowledge, the equation becomes "my students know things → I am noticing that they don't know or care about the things I need them to for my curriculum to land → what's wrong with the curriculum?" The desirable behavior is noticing that there is a mismatch and becoming curious about it.

The following is an example of a specific mismatch, playing out on a fairly large scale. As mentioned previously, I was an administrator in a high performing network of public charter schools, responsible for the curriculum and assessment program. Chicago Public Schools implemented an assessment of biliteracy (which was meant to serve as a pathway to the State Seal of Biliteracy) for fifth- and eighth-grade students. The students that I served were predominantly Latinx, many of whom were bilingual, albeit at various levels of proficiency. I proposed that eligible students in our schools take the assessment, guessing that many would do well, earn the medal, and be invited to the ceremony celebrating their biliteracy. Many of my colleagues declined, suggesting their students were not proficient Spanish speakers and would likely do poorly on the assessment. I changed my original position, which had been allowing schools to opt in, to insisting that all eligible fifth- and eighth-grade students take the assessment. Even if the scores weren't what we might hope, we would generate useful data that we could use to improve the Spanish language arts classes we offered in our schools. As results came back, we discovered that the overwhelming majority of our students were indeed biliterate, according to this assessment. Students were invited to a citywide celebration of biliteracy, rewarded for knowledge and skills that their parents may have been punished for. Our students had tremendous language knowledge that was invisible to many educators, as it had never before been relevant or associated with something that we valued. Not only that, but many of my colleagues had posited that this large body of student knowledge did not even exist. There had been a mismatch between what our students knew and what our schools were held accountable for and hence trained professionals to care about.

The example of biliteracy is specific enough that it is difficult to transfer to the development of culturally sustaining curriculum. But it illustrates an important dynamic and may surface a necessary mind-set shift for designers in this process. It is far better to assume that students hold knowledge that we have not been trained to see or value, understanding that students use the knowledge they have to access new information, build new knowledge, and develop new skills, than to assume they do not have it at all.

There is a well-loved study that points to students' ability to use background knowledge to access texts, even when their reading proficiency might suggest otherwise.[2] Students across a spectrum of reading proficiency levels were asked to read a text about a baseball game. The study found that students who were familiar with baseball were better able to read and comprehend the text than those who were not familiar, regardless of their reading level. This study is often referenced in discussions on the importance of background knowledge and how it can be used by students to engage challenging texts. It has also been misapplied to suggest that background knowledge is more important than teaching reading comprehension strategies. I consider this study a salient example of a generalizable principle: students can use their familiarity with a topic to take on rigorous academic tasks. Familiarity advantages a student, and students lacking familiarity are at a disadvantage—just as I would be reading *any* text about baseball, even as an educated adult.

Designers ought not attempt to discover their students' "baseball." We acknowledge that we have been trained to be blind to much of the knowledge our students have. Many also cringe when recalling well-meaning educators' attempts to design learning experiences that they believed would tap into students' prior knowledge, based on a superficial understanding. Rap lyrics about the US Constitution and endless basketball-related math problems leap to mind. We also cannot turn to students to clue us in on what background knowledge they can bring to bear, as they are children. Designers can do two things with this understanding. The first is to confront any *"Ay Bendito* syndrome" (an expression of pity) that lingers from past experience, affecting their beliefs about or expectations of their students' knowledge.[3] The second is to remain curious about what knowledge students possess and will use to access and interact with the projects they are designing, resting on the research-based conclusion that students' lives and communities have equipped them with knowledge that will be useful in their academic pursuits whenever and wherever the academic program makes that possible.

While the first and second takeaway are both clear, neither is actionable enough for designers to make difficult decisions regarding content—that is, what to include and what to leave out. For more actionable information, we look not backward in time at what students have learned that they can use, but forward in time to 1) what students are owed, and 2) how they respond when they get it. For the former, we will explore a phrase that has become a common refrain among learned people of color when discussing their educational experiences: "I had never even heard of _____ until I was in college." For the latter, we will examine the social-emotional impacts on students when people they identify with are well represented in the curriculum.

Students Are Owed a Knowledge of Their Own History

It has been my experience, when talking with small groups of learned and wise people of color about this work, that a certain phrase crops up repeatedly. That phrase is some version of "I had never even heard of _____ until I was in college." When one person surfaces this topic, most other participants in the conversation nod knowingly, and then share their own version of that phrase. In a mixed-generation group, these statements from the older participants often astonish the younger. In such conversations, I have heard, "I had never even heard of Mexican repatriation until I was in college," "I'd never heard of Harvey Milk until I was in college," "I had never read a Latino author until I was in college," and "I had never read a Black author before college." This conversation can go on and on, broaching topics that are nuanced but important, and shedding light on students' future potential challenges living in a world in which injustice is real. This conversation also surfaces the plain and simple erasure of Black and brown voices from curriculum, which was comprehensive or nearly complete before the 1990s. Some progress has been made with regard to improving representation, particularly in language arts curriculum. These "I had never even heard of" phrases are laments. They call out what adults now know they would have benefited from when they were young. They are lamenting an adult understanding of what they as students were owed and were denied.

Designers of curriculum cannot ensure, with a single project or even a handful, that students will be cultivated in the intellectual tradition of their community. For that goal to be met would require systems-level changes affecting students' educational experiences from early years through graduation, touching curriculum, preservice training for teachers, public policy around school accountability, and funding. It is true that single projects can eliminate an "I never heard of" statement in the future. Designers do have the power to introduce information that they believe to be critical, fundamental, or owed to students.

The information that students are owed relating to the project being written is sometimes made clear by instructional mandates. I, for instance, was unaware of Mexican repatriation in the 1930s until Illinois passed an instructional mandate, requiring that this history be taught in schools. This prompted me to include this topic in curriculum to be developed for schools serving largely Mexican American communities. This information may be foundational knowledge that the designer has and is building upon as they explore complex themes and ideas. It is important to recognize this foundational knowledge as potentially new to students and teachers who will use this project, and to dedicate the time and attention necessary for that content to land. Lastly, the information that students are owed may also have surfaced during the designer's discovery process. It's not uncommon for designers, in the course of the design process, to encounter information that both is new to them and seems important for students to know.

Designers should begin to zero in on the information that they want students to know as a result of participating in the unit of study being designed. It is helpful to imagine students many years in the future, and what they might remember about the project. It is unlikely that most will remember the authentic question, but we hope they will remember being engaged in dynamic classroom discourse or an inspiring demonstration of knowledge. It is more likely that students may one day say, "I remember doing a project *about* _____." In thinking about content, designers should be able to say what exactly they hope students remember, like many of us remember that we read the *Odyssey*, had to learn about the US Constitution, or memorized the periodic table. This is the phase of the design process where designers should decide how students might complete that sentence, knowing exactly what will come after "a project about."

Representation Develops Students' Self-Concept

There is much to be gained in selecting content that allows students to see reflections of themselves or their community in the curriculum. When students' identities and communities are reflected in the curriculum, there are positive social-emotional benefits. Students are able to form a healthy self-concept when they are exposed to role models with whom they identify, including both people with whom they can actually interact and those featured in literature and history presented by the curriculum.

Studies across racial and ethnic groups have found a strong correlation between students' positive identification with their racial or ethnic identity and academic performance.[4] For students who identified poorly with their racial or ethnic identity, indicators of success in school—like grades, test scores, and attendance—trended downward.[5] These studies have been done primarily in schools that offered ethnic studies curriculum designed to cohere to the identities of the students they served (Black studies in schools with predominantly Black students, Latinx studies in schools serving predominantly Latinx students). In these contexts, students were engaged in studying history and literature from communities associated with their racial or ethnic identity. This increased students' positive academic self-concept as learners, academic motivation, and sense of agency related to their ability to navigate a racially hostile world.

Sustained curricular attention to the histories and literature from Black and Latinx communities that also address issues of oppression and marginalization had positive effects on Black and Latinx students' senses of communalism, belonging, and self as an "academic insider." This strengthening of marginalized students' academic enfranchisement and sense of the relevance of school is a predictable outcome when schools invest the time and resources necessary to develop materials and train teachers on both their use and purpose.

Interestingly, White students in one of these studies reported difficulty dealing with the loss of authority and agency to drive classroom-based conversation, which they attributed to their lacking connection to the authors and characters presented in the curriculum. This experience of being an academic outsider (or experiencing academic disenfranchisement) for students from the dominant group is another expression of the privilege of familiarity, manifested as surprise by students from the dominant group when they could not access that privilege.[6]

There Is Nothing Specifically Beneficial About the Canon

This section is not meant to indict the traditional canon and certainly not to disparage the good people who teach it. Rather, it is meant to free designers from the self-imposed constraints that come from our own attachments to that canon. In order to do so, and to fully understand what features of the curriculum have what benefits, it is important to critically examine the relationship the curriculum has with the traditional canon. This step looms large for many designers and deserves special attention. A designer's attachment to the canon has a powerful effect in undermining their efforts in developing materials centered on nondominant narratives and hidden histories. It is a natural tendency to gravitate toward content that a designer is familiar with. This tendency is strengthened by beliefs that students ought to know what we know, that well-formed minds will resemble our own, and that choices that depart significantly from the things that we know and understand will have negative effects on our students. These tendencies will not serve the design process well, so we address them to better position ourselves to make choices that will serve our projects.

In this phase of the unit's evolution, designers are prone to taking new learnings from their discovery process or articulation of questions that are authentic to the community of focus and steering the arc of the inquiry back toward content they know well, are familiar with, and are comfortable teaching. When this happens, the design process has served only to put a culturally relevant veneer on an otherwise traditional product.

This hearkens back to chapter 1's discussion of the line of thinking that "culturally relevant teaching is not about the picture, it's about the frame," which suggests that there was never anything wrong with the original picture, only the way that it was framed. For teachers, this would mean there is nothing wrong with what has been taught in the past, only that it has lacked a culturally relevant "hook." The endgame of both of these mindsets amounts to trickery—tricking non-White students into engaging with traditional histories or literature, and ultimately avoiding having to make the fundamental and necessary shifts ourselves.

While most designers in this process would already have rid themselves of this explicit thinking, the natural tendency to gravitate toward familiar content can have similar results. In order to prevent designers from steering projects back toward dominant narratives by selecting familiar content, I sometimes shine a bright light on our attachment to the canon with provocative statements like "No one needs Shakespeare." If our task is to teach the skills outlined in modern standards, such as integration of knowledge and ideas, Shakespeare is no more useful than Audre Lorde or Toni Morrison. If our goal is for students to master chronological reasoning and causation, the French Revolution is no more useful than the US Bracero Program.

Language arts and social science standards have both undergone significant revision, and subsequent shifts in curriculum and instruction have been the subject of much research in the last decade. While in development, both Common Core language arts standards and the C3 Framework for Social Science Standards had to address political as well as learning science considerations. These frameworks had to be both sound and politically viable, leading to pedagogically crisp and content-agnostic frameworks. Those writing both standards sets were nationally recognized education researchers and experts, who doubtlessly labored over the learning science behind, wording of, and potential applications for each and every standard. Both the language arts and social science standards focused on skills that the writers believed would lead to students' success in college, career, and life outside of school. They likely also understood that specifying content to pair with those skills would make national adoption improbable.

The research that followed changes to these standards sets and the subsequent shifts to curriculum and instruction gave rise to debate about the role of skill-based instruction and what role content should play. Knowledge of this debate and these schools of thought may prompt designers to wonder where this design process is positioned in those arguments. It is not my interest to insert myself into the discussion of the correct interpretation of language arts or social studies standards. It is important to note, however, that it would be easy to extrapolate my statements about the importance of content and building background knowledge to the content that the implementers personally value. This would be a misinterpretation of my argument. There is no research to suggest that departing from the traditional canon of content has detrimental effects. There is no research to support that students benefit from a steady diet of canonical content, either. There *is* much research to suggest that building students' background knowledge is an important input for skill development, but nothing stating that a traditional interpretation of "background knowledge" benefits students. All of this is to reiterate that those seeking to teach chronological reasoning and causation are no better off referring to the French Revolution than the US Bracero Program. Students won't master the skills more quickly, nor will they need background knowledge about the French Revolution more in the future. In fact, likely the opposite: if one set of historical events is equally well set up to teach a skill (say, chronological reasoning) as the canonical example, the question of content selection then comes down to which will be more relevant to students' previous and future lived experiences. Compare the storming of the Bastille in 1789 and the Mexican Labor Agreement, which set the stage for forcible removal of American citizens of Mexican descent in the 1954 (through Operation Wetback, which, though hard to believe, is the action's legal and official name). One set of events better allows students to draw connections from classroom learning to their lived experiences, and from historical themes to highly relevant modern conditions, than does the other. One set of events presents a better opportunity to address the deficits created by the system, described by the phrase "I had never even heard of _____ until I went to college." We could argue that students are owed one information set, whereas the other might seem less critical to their preparedness for college, career, and a civically engaged life.

None of this is to say that Shakespeare is detrimental to students. There have certainly been "lightbulb moments" in classrooms where Shakespeare was being taught. Rather, it is to say that there are a fixed number of instructional minutes in a student's life in school. Those minutes historically have been dedicated to what this process refers to as "the traditional canon." As we come to understand that students benefit from, flourish with, and are owed information and narratives that are not part of the traditional canon, we recognize that those resources will take instructional minutes away from that canon. We must lean into this choice and be highly critical of tendencies that draw us into a "both and" scenario. Students are owed a focused and unapologetic examination of their hidden histories and intellectual tradition. We ought not take instructional minutes away from that pursuit.

Content for the New Canon

The choices that designers will make now are a level or two higher than what might be expected or intuited as a next step. A *learning objective* describes what students will know or be able to do at the end of a project or course, and is often assessed through the demonstration of an observable skill (typically grounded in a standard). A level higher (or broader) than learning objectives are *enduring understandings*, which speak to a core idea or process that connects the content being studied within the discipline to life outside of the classroom. What designers will describe next is a level higher still: *positing an addition to the canon, or a component of a new canon.*

By recognizing that the content that will benefit our students has been excluded from the traditional canon, and identifying content that we believe our students are owed, we are making a statement about the traditional canon when we choose the content that will be the focus of our projects. We are both calling out a deficit in the canon and recommending an addition to or reformulation of it.

An example can be found in Annabeth's work. In her research, Annabeth discovered that the topic of reparations is both a prominent theme in history and highly relevant today. In conversation with the scholar supporting her design work, it became clear that this topic was weighty enough to warrant significant discussion for her students. Annabeth did not choose to write a project about the Reconstruction period generally (a canonical topic) and include discussion of reparations. In choosing to write a project *about reparations,* Annabeth both calls out that this important topic is not addressed in the canon and posits that it should be part of the canon, as evidenced by gravitas of her project—or, perhaps more importantly, that reparations is a topic that is part of the Black American canon, is relevant to the Black intellectual tradition, and should be taught in schools.

For this step, designers should review their authentic question or questions articulated in the previous step and reflect on the following:

- What content should students be conversant with in order to respond to these questions?
- What opportunities are created by these questions to present students with critical information?
- What information is unlikely to be presented to students elsewhere?

Designers' responses ought to be concrete, not thematic or esoteric. They should refer to specific historical events, literature, and people. They should be too concrete and specific to be usable as an enduring understanding. If a designer were working on an inquiry that addressed reparations, an example would be "Bills proposing monetary reparations payments were first brought to Congress in the 1860s and have continued to be periodically thereafter." A nonexample, focused on a historical theme, would be "Reparations for slavery is an ongoing struggle." The designer should generate several similar statements, outlining the facts, histories, or information sets that students will draw upon to arrive at their own answer to the authentic question.

Stems for these statements could include:

- Timelines describing _____
- The poetry of _____; the writings or essays of _____
- Historical events surrounding _____ and _____

These statements can refer to different types of information, including literature, data sets, and historical documents. They could span multiple time periods. Keep these notes for future reference, as they will be useful when you begin to select sources.

The example in table 5.1, from a previous project inspired by the work of Sandra Cisneros, includes a description of the topic, the authentic ques-

TABLE 5.1 *Authentic question with theme and anchoring content for the Cisneros project*

Authentic question: Does my language determine where I belong?	
Theme	*Students will know*
Language as a cultural identifier has been used to group and divide people throughout US history, consistently and acutely for Spanish speakers.	Literary works by Sandra Cisneros; history of US English-only policies, timelines, and demographics of Spanish speakers in US beginning in the 1500s

tion, and the content that was identified for students to anchor on in investigating the question. The project examines ways bilingualism is both celebrated and continues to be stigmatized or punished in modern society, posing the question "Does my language determine where I belong?" Cisneros, among the first prominent US authors to weave together Spanish and English to explore the complexities of growing up bilingual/bicultural, addresses this theme in her works. Students investigate the ways US society has compounded these complexities by punishing certain bilingualism in both subtle and overt ways. Students are asked to respond to the question of whether bilingualism builds belonging by strengthening ties to one's community and culture, or disrupts belonging to the larger community because of stigma. The distilled product of the process of determining what content should be added to the canon, and the content that the designers chose to center in this project, is articulated under "Students will know."

Examples from the Design Cohort

Malika

Malika's conversations with Dr. Ralph surfaced the opportunity to highlight contemporary Eritrean diaspora leaders, most notably Nipsey Hussle, a hip-hop artist and community leader who was killed in Los Angeles in 2019. Dr. Ralph felt strongly that Nipsey Hussle represented the leadership characteristics and values that would be presented through the study of King Ashama, and that this contemporary example would reinforce the model of Eritrean leadership central to the project.

Dr. Ralph also suggested that Eritrean leaders have distinctive ways to make decisions within their communities. His description accorded with

Malika's experience of seeing family members and community leaders employ these methods, which are part arbitration and part pastoral care. Dr. Ralph referred to the methods as "indigenous community deliberations," and suggested that they point to a fundamentally different approach to and conception of leadership. This lens seemed highly relevant and resonated with Malika as an important learning for students from both African diaspora and other communities. Malika determined that what students should know by the end of the project are historical and contemporary model Eritrean leaders, and the fact that communities make decisions in various ways, including the methods for deliberation that she herself had witnessed and Dr. Ralph gave language to in their discussion.

Cam

Cam surfaced cases that substantively changed individuals' rights within relationships. *Obergefell v. Hodges* (2015) overturned *Baker*, requiring that all states issue marriage licenses to LGBT couples. *Kirchberg v. Feenstra* (1981) found unconstitutional a Louisiana Head and Master Law assigning all marital property rights to the husband. *Loving vs. Virginia* struck down laws banning interracial marriage. In all these cases, social realities contributed to these significant legal changes. It is also true that social realities changed as a result of these new laws.

Cam wanted students to know that what we now know as equalities were not always so. In many cases these equalities were the result of both social and legal changes. This also suggests that there are equalities that still require social realities to change and laws to be changed. Cam hoped to equip students with this knowledge by presenting cases that led to what are now held as important social equalities, such as women's right to property and LGBTQ rights to marry. He also hoped to situate these cases within the social context of the day (attitudes, representation, public opinion) to surface the interplay between legal and social change.

David

David concluded, based on his research and consultation with a scholar, that generational trauma in marginalized communities has significant, in some cases daily, impacts on students' lives, and that discussion of these dynamics is almost entirely absent from the curriculum. David believed that students were owed knowledge of and language to describe marginalized communities in modern society and the reality of generational trauma.

Knowledge of ways that communities respond also came through as key—it is valuable to know that communities respond to marginalization and traumatizing events in a variety of ways that are empowering and hopeful.

Annabeth

Throughout her discovery process Annabeth gathered information, much of which was not unknown to her but was more compelling when organized to tell the story around discussions of reparations. These included accounts from enslaved people; analyses of the economic value added by Black and brown peoples in the colonial era; and various, ultimately unsuccessful, efforts throughout US history toward making reparations payments. Annabeth felt that these histories, presented appropriately, would demystify the controversy around reparations that was showing up regularly in political discourse, which many students did not have the information necessary to access.

Annabeth also saw merit in students' knowledge of contemporary efforts to make reparations, not only on national political stages but by organizations and state governments. It seemed valuable that students know that reparations are possible and see the effects they have, when successful, on both the direct beneficiaries and the communities that chose to make them.

CHAPTER 6

Developing Bold Voices

Demonstrations of Knowledge

In the previous chapter, designers determined what content students would interact with in order to respond to the authentic question for their project. In this chapter, designers will return to the question of authenticity as they design the demonstration of knowledge, or final performance task, that reflects the intellectual tradition of their community of focus. Designers will examine different *ways of knowing*, or demonstrating that one knows something, and how these can vary among groups of people. In order to be thoughtful about this element of their projects, designers will also consider how demonstrations of knowledge have the potential to instill or erode a sense of agency in students.

Various Ways of Knowing: Epistemologies for Marginalized Communities

Previous chapters have featured lengthy discussion of intellectual traditions. Students come from communities that have an intellectual tradition all their own, made up of histories, literature, poetry, art, and more. A feature of these intellectual traditions is their *epistemologies*. This word refers to a community's philosophy of knowledge—that is, how one discerns the difference between opinion and fact, what counts as evidence, and, more broadly, "how you know when you know."

The idea that K–12 education puts forth a single intellectual tradition as valid and worthy of study has also been a focus in previous chapters. Just as K–12 education centers on an intellectual tradition and the histories, literature, poetry, and art that make up the traditional canon, it also has a specific and well-codified set of epistemologies. This set of epistemologies is established by the standards, but is crystallized in a narrow interpretation of those standards. The traditional canon is held and adhered to by a system that is standardized, but the canon itself is not standardized. The canon is not the focus of the standards, or of standardization generally. This is also true of epistemologies. The skills that students are to master are standardized and represented by standards, but the ways in which students demonstrate mastery are not standardized. The narrowness of interpretation comes from our attachment to a set of epistemologies with which we are familiar. Just as we have taken steps to be critical of the choices that come out of our attachment to the familiar regarding the authenticity of our questions, and the content students may use to answer them, it is important now to acknowledge our attachments to the epistemologies that undergird our design of demonstrations of knowledge.

For designers who have done the work to discover for themselves the heroes and heroines from the communities they are writing for, discern those protagonists' questions to society today, and determine what information students are owed to explore those questions, the idea of authentic expressions of knowledge will not be surprising. If questions can be authentic to a community or not, it stands to reason that expressions of knowledge could be equally authentic or inauthentic. To be well positioned to make design choices that will serve the authenticity of the demonstration of knowledge, many designers will benefit from a more thorough examination of this feature of the curriculum.

Epistemology, more than content knowledge, presents the possibility for a mismatch between the intellectual tradition that students are being cultivated in outside of the classroom and what is required of them inside classrooms. Students hear elders demonstrate their knowledge frequently. These same patterns of expression are mirrored by other community and family members. For some students, the classroom is another venue in which they can practice and hone their skills of demonstration without significant adjustments. For others, the adjustment is significant; in those cases, the student carries an additional cognitive load when demonstrating what they know and can do, which points to a clear inequity in the system. Mark practices the same demonstration of knowledge in and out of school, but Kelly practices different demonstrations of knowledge in and out of school, and must select the right epistemology to employ at the right time. There are more steps for Kelly, more complexity for her to navigate.

For some students, the difference is as clear as language. In church and at home students hear elders and parents make sense of the world and participate in that meaning-making in one language. In school, students are required to hear and participate in meaning-making in a different language, inclusive of all of the vocabulary, patterns of speech, and colloquialisms associated with that language.

For many students, the difference is more subtle but still significant. Even where the language of expression is the same, the patterns of meaning-making and the evidence that counts as valid in that meaning-making might be quite different. How does one construct an argument? Does one's personal experience count as evidence? Many students are practiced in an epistemology that is valid in their home and community lives, but invalid in the context of their schooling. This sets up an inequity, privileging students whose home- and community-based practices around demonstrating knowledge are consistent with their schooling, while disadvantaging others. While some students are adept at navigating multiple expressions of knowledge, for most this dynamic is confounding, frustrating, and potentially damaging.

Mismatching Knowledge Systems: A Personal Account

In order to make this point less hazy or theoretical and to provide more clarity, I will share my own personal experience with this dynamic.

I grew up in the church. My father was a pastor and preacher. He is well educated and thoroughly steeped in the mainline Protestant intellectual tradition. Uncles, great-uncles, and grandparents were also pastors and preachers. Our community life was largely made up of weeknights in the church, surrounded by church members and their families. Many of our friends were pastors of other churches. I was immersed in a community that valued speaking in a clear and compelling way, had both formal and informal mechanisms for building these skills, and took a codified approach to meaning-making, which emphasized allegory.

I was well served by this home- and community-based knowledge system in my primary and secondary schooling. I had a good vocabulary, and spoke with confidence and poise. I even won speech competitions in primary school. The communication skills were valued in my schooling, and the epistemology hadn't bumped into anything because it was close enough to the school-based epistemology to be acceptable.

This was not true in graduate school, where I studied both in a school of education and a business school. There was a clear yet unstated epistemology in both contexts, which was most visible to me when I was asked questions by professors. When professors asked me questions, I leaned on the skills and tendencies that had been built in my community. I began answering questions with a story or experience, where I would surface a theme or principle. I would connect the principle that I had surfaced in the story to the principle I thought was most relevant to the question, and would then bridge to answering the question and cite evidence that supported my position.

I quickly learned that professors did not like this, and I internalized the message that I did not know how to answer questions appropriately in graduate school. I came to understand that my professors were looking for a fundamentally different type of response; allegory was not acceptable evidence or welcomed information. This was very problematic for me, because in my community, starting with a story is *the thing*, and the ability to do so well separated the proverbial sheep from the goats. My professors were interested in my answer, my evidence, maybe an application. Some of my classmates had this approach down cold. I came to believe that I needed to learn how to respond to questions appropriately, like someone who belonged in grad school and, in my career that followed, like someone who had been to grad school.

Both during my studies and in the years that followed, I practiced responding to questions using the approach that I had learned to be correct. When asked a question, I would supply an answer first, followed by evidence or grounding for my reasoning, and end with a potential application of that logic chain. The only problem was that even after years of practice responding to questions "correctly," I was not very good at it. My responses were consistently faltering. My mind would still look for an allegory to make my point more resonant. I would often start with a direct response which I found to be unconvincing, stop in the middle of my argument and say, "Let me start over," and then introduce an allegory that would ultimately allow me to make my point in a way that made sense. Having learned to second-guess my preferences in expressing my ideas made me a worse communicator.

This example is situated in a privileged context. Both my home-based knowledge system and the graduate school knowledge system are privileged in our society. My parents and many community members were well-educated people. This is evidenced by the fact that my home-based knowledge system served me well until grad school. The context in which that epistemology was devalued was in graduate school, which is also a privileged context. The question designers might now ask is, "If this example of mismatch between even privileged epistemologies ends in self-doubt and erosion of agency, how much more acute and negative are the effects for people whose ways of knowing explicitly devalued?" My experience is a light example, but hopefully clear enough that designers can transfer this principle when considering the experiences of students who disproportionately get the red pen when they express their ideas or demonstrate their knowledge in ways most natural to them.

Many professional educators have experience with students who are able to navigate both home- and school-based systems of meaning-making with fluency. We often wonder how some students are able to engage well in two or more knowledge systems while others have a more difficult time. This may bring discussions of code-switching to mind. Those familiar with the broader conversation around code-switching, and techniques that have been posited to supposedly support students in developing these skills, might wonder why the focus of this chapter is development of authentic demonstrations of knowledge rather than development of code-switching skills. Don't all students need to develop these skills?

The answer to this question is resoundingly no. Not all students need to develop code-switching skills. Those skills are situated outside of the curriculum, meaning they are not articulated in standards, and it is only in the interpretation of the standards that the individuals in the system determine who needs or does not need to learn code-switching skills. Were code-switching a curricular issue, all students and teachers would be held accountable to it. Were this the case, middle-class White students would be required to represent their ideas in sociolinguistic styles (sets of linguistic variants with social meaning) not their own, which would be a rare phenomenon, in my experience.

No, indeed only certain students have this demand placed on them, and that group is exclusively poor and predominantly non-White. Designers may come to their own conclusions about the place code-switching has in their schools according to their own judgment. What should be clear from a design process perspective is that prior efforts to situate projects within the intellectual tradition of the community being written for should also apply to the summative demonstration of knowledge. Subtle decisions in this phase of the design process can lead to learning experiences that encourage integration in students' ways of knowing and means of expression, such that students are not asked to hold back their linguistic tools but to "bring them forcefully and strategically forward."[1]

Teaching Students to "Take Up Space"

Some may define "taking up space" as not leveraging one's best effort toward the task at hand, but rather hanging around simply "taking up space." Women, and women of color in particular, have repurposed this phrase in recent years and assigned it new meaning in certain circles. The new use of this phrase recognizes the ways that women of color have been taught to make themselves physically smaller, quiet their voices, and otherwise diminish their presence in mixed company. The response the new definition encourages, eloquently articulated by *Shine* columnist Martha Tesema, is to "take up space" physically, verbally, and intellectually in order to "walk into a room and know deep down that you belong."[2]

Demonstrations of knowledge can be designed in such a way that students' sense of agency is eroded. In these cases, sources of information are far from them, ways of knowing are foreign to them, and their own perspective is irrelevant. The information that needs to be referenced is from a distant place, time, or culture and is available only in a static format. The ways students are expected to present their learning are prescribed and patterned on dominant epistemology, which has too often become a formulaic approach to making evidence-based arguments, citing sources representing the dominant perspective as presented in the formal curriculum. Lastly, there is a predetermined correct interpretation of the information put forth.

Demonstrations of knowledge can also be designed in ways that contribute to a student's sense of agency and support the development of a positive academic self-concept, however. This is possible when sources of information are near to them or drawn from their own community. Ways of knowing can be made familiar or modeled by figures that represent their community's perspectives. Students' points of view can be treated as valuable and contribute to their demonstration of knowledge. These features of the assessment can support students' academic self-concept, which is strongly correlated with future academic achievement.[3]

It is the aim of this component of the curriculum that students might practice referring to their own communities as rich with information, their own epistemologies—whether those be oral histories, narratives represented visually in public art, or *testimonio* gathered by the students themselves—as valid, and their interpretations and perspectives as worthy of discussion. These being important inputs for a student's positive academic self-concept, the desired outcome is that students grow into a knowing of their belonging in academic spaces and their comfort taking up space in those rooms.

Demonstration of Knowledge

With the guidance and support of a scholar or elder from the community they are writing for, designers should review the authentic questions they have articulated. They should now also return to the content they believe students deserve to know and will need in order to respond to the authentic

question. Designers are now invited to read the following questions and
take notes on their ideas in response to these questions:

- What "ways of knowing" or demonstrations of knowledge might
  naturally show up in sources for this project?
- What local, home-, or community-based information could students
  use as evidence as a part of their response?
- How might students put themselves into their responses? Where might
  students share their point of view, informed by their experience?

The next step is to design a final demonstration of knowledge in which
students will refer to the information presented to them throughout the
course of the project and respond to the authentic question. As designers
sketch this demonstration of knowledge, they should draw on the ideas
they just noted relating to the preceding questions. The demonstration of
knowledge should meet the following criteria:

- Be a response to the authentic question
- Represent the student's position
- Draw on relevant evidence in support of their position
- Acknowledge opposing views, where the format is argumentative
  (which need not always be the case)

Before beginning to sketch a demonstration of knowledge that meets
these criteria, we will return to the first prompt: What "ways of knowing"
or demonstrations of knowledge might naturally show up as sources in
this project? Projects naturally present epistemology in the sources that
are presented. When students study prominent Black leaders or orators,
those leaders are presenting a way of knowing and demonstrating their
knowledge through their speech. The structure and unique characteristics
of the speeches constitute an epistemology with roots in the "folk pulpit."[4]
Where students might study Latinx artists using certain techniques or imagery, those artists are demonstrating their knowledge as a visual epistemology.[5] Where students are studying LGBTQ activists, the legal actions
they review present a way that those leaders engage in sense-making and
present their ideas. Source selection will take place in later steps, but the
theme and content that designers have selected can point to the emerging
epistemology of the inquiry. Designers can make educated guesses as to

the types of sources that will be relevant based on their chosen theme and content, and extrapolate the emerging epistemology of the project.

This approach prevents designers from having to know or learn epistemology that is not their own and apply that elusive knowledge to the design of their demonstration of knowledge. *Allow the heroes, heroines, and protagonists that the project is organized around to reveal an authentic demonstration of knowledge.* When sources are selected, further analysis will be required to ensure that the epistemology is reflected in the design of the prompts, and that those are clear and crisp. For example, if designers decide to anchor on prominent Black orators and their speeches as the emergent epistemology for their project, those designers will need to analyze the speeches used as sources and refer to their format in order to design prompts such that the epistemology shows up in students' work.

Designers should note the possible formats for students' demonstration of knowledge based on the emergent epistemology of the project. The second prompt, "What local, home-, or community-based information could students use as evidence as a part of their response?" asks designers to reflect on what assets students might have access to and consider those assets coequal to those the project has presented. These assets should be separate from the students' perspective, but should be information that the student is able to independently gather. What data sets might students use to make connections between a historical theme and their local community? This might include demographic data, ways national issues are taking shape locally, or ways subgroups that students identify with are impacted. What community or family members might students interview in order to cite firsthand accounts or *testimonio* in their responses? Treating home- and community-based knowledge as a valid source will be discussed in the following chapter, but should be considered in this phase. What experts or leaders might be available for a discussion with the class, or might provide written replies to questions that could be cited in students' responses? While some firsthand experiences may be too rare or delicate for students to conduct interviews individually, whole-group dialogue with community members can produce valuable information for students' use.

Designers should note possible sources of information students will draw on beyond provided resources in their responses, and consider the third prompt: "How might students put themselves into their responses?

Where might students share their point of view, informed by their experience?" How will students be invited to put themselves into their responses? This is not to suggest that every demonstration of knowledge becomes an op-ed. It is important, however, to prompt students to identify themselves, their connection to the topic, and personal experiences that inform their position. Their personhood is important. It is a critical element of designing demonstrations of knowledge that encourage students to take up space in the room, and it is also the simplest. Students may surface experiences or components of their personhood that are highly relevant to the topic, and they may not. In either case, being prompted to "put yourself in your response" engenders an ethic of dignity. That students are asked to identify themselves in their responses suggests that they expect to be seen and known, which undergirds the expectation that they will be heard.

Designers can sketch the final demonstration of knowledge by completing the following statements:

- "Students will produce a _____." This might be a speech, photo essay, op-ed, or interview-based article, reflecting the epistemology of the project and grounded in a way of knowing that is authentic to the community.
- "Students will respond to the authentic question, citing relevant sources to support their position, including _____." Local impact data relevant to the topic, firsthand accounts, or quotes and perspective from local leaders are possibilities.
- "Students may share their personal experiences or ways their identity informs their perspective."

Table 6.1 shows a partial map of a demonstration of learning in this format from previous work, including a brief description of the topic, the organizing (authentic) question, and the content (sources) students reviewed. This project, inspired by Sor Juana Inés de la Cruz, a colonial era Mexican poet and protofeminist, asked students to respond to the question, "Is gender a source or limitation of power?" The project set up a schema by which students would analyze various people's sources of power (legitimate, referential, informational, expert, coercive, and reward). Students identified when those sources of power were associated with traditional gender roles

TABLE 6.1 *Partial map for Sor Juana Inés de la Cruz unit*

Authentic question: Do gender roles provide or limit power?	
Theme	*Students will know*
All people have different sources of power, some of which are associated with gender roles, which change because of individual actions and social context (time, place).	The writings of protofeminist, prolific poet Sor Juana Inés de la Cruz; five power bases within and outside the home; demographic information on gender and societal roles

Note on epistemology: Testimonio—a first-person narrative that gives voice to a shared or common experience for a group rarely given the opportunity for written account

Demonstration of knowledge: Students will conduct interview/gather testimonio from women in their lives and provide analysis on their sources of power. Students will respond to the question, "Do gender roles provide or limit power?" citing evidence supporting their position and identifying sources and limitations of power in testimonio, both provided and conducted. Students may identify personal experiences or ways that their identity informs their position.

in various time periods, and when and why people choose to step outside of traditional gender roles to have the power they need to survive or thrive. The project centered on Latinas and their experience of gender and power, including expressions of gender roles and power in different time periods. The sources provided to students were firsthand accounts (e.g., essays written by Sor Juana Inés de la Cruz, interviews with first- and second-generation college students, and vignettes portraying Latinx men taking on child-rearing responsibilities).

At the end of this step, designers will have articulated their organizing question ("Authentic question") and the historico-cultural (relating to cultural history) theme students will explore ("Theme"), determined the content that students are owed and will serve as an anchor to their response ("Students will know"), outlined the epistemology of the project ("Note on epistemology"), and designed a final demonstration of knowledge centered on that way of knowing ("Demonstration of knowledge"), requiring students to gather relevant information and put their perspective, rooted in their personhood, into their response.

Examples from the Design Cohort

Malika

Malika considered what sources might be useful to respond to the question, "What does the way a nation treats immigrants say about its leaders?" While policy is one way that leaders make their position known, neither of the Eritrean leaders to be presented would have demonstrated his sense-making through policy documents. The community deliberations described by Dr. Ralph represented a different process for decision-making, and a different means of representing those decisions.

Malika determined that rhetoric would be a consistent means of expression across the various leaders the project would present in resources. Both Eritrean and Western leaders would make their values and model of leadership known, and these could be pinpointed and examined via their rhetoric.

Malika's draft is shown in table 6.2.

TABLE 6.2 *Malika's emerging project map*

Authentic question: What does the way a nation treats immigrants say about its leaders?	
Theme Eritreans/Ethopians have care for others as a key value relating to leadership, as distinct from some Western models of leadership.	*Students will know* King Ashama and his leadership inform Eritrean cultural values including care for immigrants; various communities have distinct methods for decision-making.
Note on epistemology: Indigenous community deliberations consider many sides of an issue and guide community members to values-based, pragmatic decisions using both mediation and pastoral care.	
Demonstration of knowledge: Students will prepare talking points to inform a response to questions from community members at a town hall regarding the treatment of immigrant communities in their city. Students will gather data on challenges faced by immigrant communities in their city in preparation. Students will represent their values and ways those values inform their position as leaders, specifically their position on care for immigrant communities.	

Cam

Cam knew that a combination of legal documents and secondary sources relating to those legal documents would likely be used as sources in his project. Representation of social realities, including examples in media of observable changes in public opinion, would also be relevant. Cam was able to have conversations with Johanna Eager, director of the Human Rights Campaign's Welcoming Schools Initiative. Eager suggested that in making LGBTQ rights issues real and accessible to schools, referring to the individual school's mission and values documents can be helpful. These documents frequently refer to creation of bully-free, inclusive spaces through "respect for all" statements. These statements about inclusion do not always refer to sexuality and may not have been crafted with LGBTQ people in mind; nonetheless, they are statements of values that create a context for conversations about equality and inclusion at the school level.

Cam determined that the epistemological lens for this project would be policy documents and the discussions they foster that extend rights to more people by changing either the application of the document (social reality changing in response to laws) or the document itself (social reality changing laws). Cam chose to focus on discourse around school or district mission statements as the place students would apply this knowledge to their own context most appropriately.

Because of the target age group for Cam's project (late elementary) and because of the age at which it is developmentally appropriate to self-disclose sexual preference as individuals, Cam chose to have students "put themselves into the project" as a class, by examining their school's position on inclusivity.

Cam's emerging project map is shown in table 6.3.

TABLE 6.3 *Cam's emerging project map*

Authentic question: What makes "equality" equal?	
Theme	*Students will know*
Social realities inform laws relating to equality, and vice versa	Landmark cases and civil rights actions establishing equality in relationships; social realities surrounding putting those actions in context

Note on epistemology: Policy documents and discourse around them	

Demonstration of knowledge: Students will review class, school, or district rules on inclusion. Students will draft a new or revised policy to propose or, if rules are adequate, create a schoolwide campaign to help other students better understand the policy.	

David

David knew that various types of sources would be necessary for students to have access to the information they needed to respond to the organizing question for his project, including secondary sources outlining historical events, scientific articles describing trauma, excerpts and interviews with artists, profiles of social justice activists and their work, and more. Given this variety, it would be difficult to parse a way of knowing that would be authentic across the sources used. David instead chose to anchor on the ways messages from artists and activists are shared with and among community members in marginalized communities, particularly youth.

David knew that his students consumed information on a variety of topics through short, shareable social media content, including the causes they cared about and artists that resonated with them. He also found it interesting that for much of this media, the topics, those profiled, and the journalists were often situated within the Black or Latinx community. He chose shareable social media or online content as the medium for students to demonstrate their knowledge, centering on the activists and artists who were responding to past and current traumas through their actions and art.

David's draft is shown in table 6.4.

TABLE 6.4 *David's emerging project map*

Authentic question: How can communities respond to generational trauma?	
Theme	*Students will know*
Traumas can be accumulated and passed down within communities, and communities have ways of responding that address both effects and causes of trauma.	The science behind generational trauma and accumulated fear; social justice movements past and present; prominent artists' depictions of traumas and ways communities benefit from these works
Note on epistemology: Shareable social media, web content particular to youth and other social movements in Black and Latinx communities	
Demonstration of knowledge: Students will produce a podcast, article-as-list, or opinion piece outlining important social justice movements, social justice activists, or artists with social purpose. A subset of those profiled will come from students' local communities. Students will use these profiles as evidence to support their response to the question, "How can communities respond to generational trauma?" Students will share their position and perspective, informed by their experiences and community life.	

Annabeth

Annabeth, like David, was not able to rely on likely sources to reveal an epistemological approach that would be authentic to the Black community she was writing for. Exploration of reparations would require a combination of historical documents both primary and secondary, sources outlining contemporary examples and their effects, as well as interviews shedding light on the controversy about and complexity of politics around reparations today. Annabeth found political speech to be the most common means of expression in contemporary sources, but also wanted to steer clear of any design that would allow her classroom to become as divisive as political discussions around reparations.

Annabeth's focus, then, was to design a demonstration of learning that would prevent arguments that would be offensive to some students and in-authentic to the ways Black historians, economists, and politicians engage with the topic.

Annabeth's draft is shown in table 6.5.

TABLE 6.5 *Annabeth's emerging project map*

Authentic question: Why are reparations controversial?	
Theme	*Students will know*
The US economy was disproportionately benefited by and under- or non-compensating of Black and brown labor. While some organizations have made reparations, larger efforts are hindered by controversy.	Application of laws to disaffect Black peoples (Jim Crow, John Punch vs. Anthony Johnson, etc.); economic realities around Black and brown labor; narratives of enslaved peoples; modern movements toward reparations, both successes and failures
Note on epistemology: *Possibly political speech, remains unclear at this stage*	
Demonstration of knowledge: Students will construct an argument (e.g., detailed outline, poster, essay) that evaluates the controversies surrounding reparations using specific claims and relevant evidence from historical and contemporary sources, while acknowledging competing views. Students will investigate local, domestic, and global examples of reparations made by governments, education institutes, or other organizations. Students will use this research to add to their response to the question, "Why are reparations controversial?"	

CHAPTER 7

Selecting Sources on the Margin

In the previous chapter, demonstrations of knowledge were designed to reflect an epistemology that is authentic to the community being written for. In this chapter, designers will select the sources that will be provided to students for responding to the project's organizing question. During this process, designers will consider a variety of source types as legitimate and useful. They will work to curate resources that maintain the position of the inquiry as situated within the intellectual tradition of the community they are writing for. Finally, designers will check the utility of resources and alignment of prompts to their organizing question by practicing responding to the question drawing on only the sources they have selected.

Whose Evidence Counts?

Finding sources that speak authentically to the questions of marginalized communities is uniquely challenging. This can be time-consuming and persnickety work, requiring long hours of searching for and discovering the not-quite-right thing—and that's when all is going well. When it does not go well, it can feel like you have been lied to; you know or believe something to be true, but when you look for confirmation, the sources that you have trusted only hide or obscure that truth. The design process might surface a historical theme that is genuine and authentic, yet the sources that can speak to the various parts of that theme are elusive and hard to find. Depending on the content a designer has chosen to center on, the narratives may have been seldom recorded, while for others those histories have been actively edited out of the record.

The question of legitimacy is an important one. As designers consider the arguments that they want students to be able to make, they should interrogate their own assumptions about what evidence they would accept as legitimate. Only primary and secondary source documents? Is literary truth considered legitimate? Can a student cite *testimonio* from their own community? Can they cite their own experiences? Does this evidence have the same weight? Why or why not?

These questions relate to the examination of epistemology in the previous chapter. Different groups of people hold different values around epistemology, and these differences are seldom more apparent than in discussions about evidence. Not only do our cultures and communities contribute to our biases, but our training does as well. Data scientists and economists have different priorities around evidence than do education researchers. Within our school systems, administrators and educators sometimes prioritize evidence of student growth differently. As it pertains to curriculum design, colleagues may have different standards for evidence in student work based on the discipline that each is trained to teach.

I advocate for categorizing projects produced by this design process as "humanities projects." There are a few reasons for this. Organizational and policy pressures have both contributed to a blurring of the line between language arts and social studies disciplines. Many school systems allocate more resources and instructional time to language arts than to the social studies in primary grades. Preservice training programs for teachers place a high priority on literacy instruction. It is also true that many language arts curricula prioritize study of nonfiction text. One reason to categorize the projects being designed as humanities projects is to accommodate these conditions. Designing units with both language arts and social studies disciplines in mind may put a larger group of teachers in a strong position to implement them. Another is to broaden the designer's palette and allow them to draw on materials from a variety of disciplines in curating sources.

The term *humanities* refers to disciplines such as languages, history, literature, philosophy, arts, and religion. These disciplines can be thought of as ways people have captured, cataloged, or documented the human experience. In K–12, this broad range of disciplines is quickly collapsed into social sciences and language arts as they concern curricula. Practically speaking, this suggests that the projects produced could be taught in either a social studies or language arts classroom. For design purposes, we will embrace the breadth of these disciplines and the many ways people have documented the human experience. This will require that the designer adopt an interdisciplinary way of thinking and apply this same lens to designing tasks and the eventual evaluation of student work.[1]

Fact Alongside Fiction

Our brains integrate information from various knowledge bases in order to make sense of our world. The work of unpacking historical and cultural themes naturally lends itself to drawing on a variety of knowledge bases. Historical knowledge, the appropriate canon of literature, an array of cultural artifacts—all are up for grabs. When one considers a question like "How will the US achieve gender equality?" a broad array of artifacts, ideas, or references rushes to mind. This could include timelines and events, depictions of the struggle for equality from books and movies, experiences from one's own personal life, and philosophy that one has been taught. If I were discussing this question with friends, we could each draw upon all of those knowledge bases to add to the conversation. When pulling from one knowledge base or another, I would make reference to the source (with statements like "In the 1930s, _____ took place" or "Have you read _____?"), which would allow for others to adjust to and understand how that information is situated in the discussion. In such a conversation, it would be difficult to control what knowledge bases were being referenced. While the goal of this work is not to diminish the distinctness of the disciplines we draw on, it is reasonable for designers to invite various disciplinary contributions to the conversation.

This way of thinking and approach to curriculum design is particularly useful for the examination of historical themes for marginalized communities. An interdisciplinary approach can add richness to the learning process, or, in some cases, it is necessary because sources from a single discipline are scarce. As libraries and collections of primary-source documents emerge in the digital space, there is still broad consensus that the experiences of people of color were underrecorded or poorly preserved. In curriculum design, it can be tricky work even with dominant narratives to surface the historical documents that will lead students to a particular understanding. This is all the more difficult when working to surface nondominant narratives.

The same historical themes that might be difficult to present using only primary- and secondary-source documents can come through clearly in literature. Poets and authors are not historians. However, they are charged with capturing a theme or idea that resonates with a particular audience or community. Oftentimes literature presents a perspective on the theme that is both authentic to the community and will resonate.

In moving toward the selection of sources for students' use, designers can begin thinking about where literature may add richness or bridge gaps left by nonfiction sources. Introducing literary figures is also a valuable opportunity to reference heroes from various sectors of community life, as discussed in chapter 2. In a project focused on LGBTQ rights, for example, students will naturally be introduced to activists. A designer might include poetry, asking students to make connections between the literary themes and the historical/social context of that poem. This will meet the primary objective of equipping students with relevant information for use in their performance task. It will also have met a secondary objective, which is introducing students to and familiarizing them with important figures excluded from the traditional canon.

Sources Situated Within an Intellectual Tradition

Like authentic questions, the sources provided to students should be situated within the intellectual tradition of the community being written for. Wherever possible, primary sources should present the voices of members of that community. Literature should be authored by members of that community. Commentary should center on, and ideally be written by, community members. It is easy to decenter the community and intellectual tradition in the selection of source material. Selecting the right sources is like setting a table for the community's elders and intellectuals to engage in deep discussion, leaving a seat open for the student.

To avoid undermining all the good work that preceded this step, it is important to revisit a key point: as with organizing questions, the bar for authenticity is whether or not an elder from within that community would cite a given resource as both credible and relevant. The questions and sources (or knowledge base) are the stuff discourse is made of. It is unlikely that elders and scholars from any community would introduce questions that are inauthentic to them or sources that wholly conflict with their perspective, much less that scholars and elders from marginalized and oppressed communities would introduce the perspective of their oppressor. The discourse should be made up of questions and sources that are consistent with the scholarly debate within that community, surfacing the tension within those questions and among those sources. To introduce elements of discourse that come from outside the community of focus would set up a cross-cultural debate on a topic of shared interest. When there is a cross-cultural debate involving dominant and nondominant communities, the thing that is most at issue is power (e.g., which community's evidence is more convincing, whose voice can dominate others'). In this scenario, where more than one community's perspective on an issue is introduced, the students' struggle is reduced to picking the side they most identify with or revealing their affiliation and building an argument to support their position. In my experience, marginalized voices stay marginalized in this equation. Struggling with cross-cultural power dynamics is at odds with the purpose of this design process. A cross-cultural examination of an issue would require an entirely different approach to design.

The sources that the designer provides establish the realm of allowable arguments. The broad goal of cultivating students within the intellectual tradition of their community has most clearly been achieved when students' responses are situated within that community. Students' responses should ideally reflect perspectives and cite sources that are authentic to the community. A student's arguments and sense-making are most likely to be reflective of only and exactly the sources provided to them. Providing sources that are authentic and situated within the intellectual tradition ensures that students' responses will follow suit.

Providing sufficiently diverse perspectives for students to be able to cite opposing views is a common concern at this stage of the process. How will students make good arguments if they are not familiar with all sides of an issue? My response to this question is that what this work is organized to do is to reproduce the privileging effects that traditional curriculum produces for the dominant group. Curriculum designed for the dominant group presents conflicting views, all of which are from the dominant group's perspective. Instances of curriculum surfacing both dominant and authentic, nondominant perspectives are few and far between. The goal, just as with traditional curricula, is to surface the tensions and diverse perspectives from within a group of scholars and experts. Designers should feel no pressure to present opposing views from outside of the community they are writing for; doing so would actually be inauthentic.

It is not uncommon for designers to include sources that outline opposing views (often not authentic to the community) so that students are able to meet criteria for making argumentative claims in their work. This presents two problems. First, presenting a source that outlines a view that is clearly in opposition to the thrust of the project dramatically reduces the rigor of the task. If students are asked to acknowledge opposing views in their responses (which is quite common), it should be somewhat difficult to do so. It should require students to struggle with real tension between credible sources that come to different conclusions. When a majority of sources build toward a given argument, presenting perspectives that students are likely to identify with, and one or two sources present an opposing and nonsympathetic view, the work of addressing opposing viewpoints becomes very easy. The examples from the design cohort in this chapter offer ways designers have navigated this area.

The second problem is that when a designer has chosen a source that presents a strongly opposing view, they have made that view an allowable argument. The sources that a designer chooses, and the classroom discourse that results, should not be polarizing or ideological in nature. It is potentially very damaging to students, particularly where engagement with nondominant perspectives or the histories of marginalized people is a goal, to introduce the possibility of ideological debate. Dominant ideologies are an instrument of marginalization. Dominant ideologies define the dominant group's perspective, and point a finger at differing perspective with the weight of the majority behind them. Dominant ideology is a bully—it's in the job description. Including sources that present dominant ideologies will marginalize the nondominant perspectives presented elsewhere in the project, and are very likely to marginalize the students who identify with them as well. Choosing sources that present dominant ideology in a project organized around nondominant narratives is like inviting a bull into a china shop. So stay safe out there, folks.

Selecting and Grouping Sources

In previous chapters, designers articulated an organizing question for their project, determined what content students will interact with, and sketched the final demonstration of knowledge. The following steps will:

- Select sources that students will need to respond to the authentic question.
- Group those sources under two to four more specific supporting questions with an associated task.

The curriculum unit will begin to take shape in this set of activities. Through selecting resources, grouping those resources, and designing tasks for students to complete, designers will flesh out their projects such that they begin to resemble instructional resources that designers are accustomed to building or using. These processes are also time-consuming and require patience, trial, and error.

Designers should begin source selection by referencing the notes they took in preparation for articulating a historico-cultural theme and determining what "students will know" in chapter 5. These notes should be completions of sentence stems like:

- "Timelines describing _____"
- "The poetry of _____, the writings or essays of _____"
- "Historical events surrounding _____, _____"

Designers should compare these and similar statements (which will be called "source notes") with the authentic question and the final demonstration of knowledge.

An example of a template for a completed unit with sources and tasks is given in table 7.1.

TABLE 7.1 *Unit template with sources and tasks*

Authentic question	
Theme	*Students will know*
Note on epistemology:	
Demonstration of knowledge	
Formative task 1	*Sources*
	• "Timelines describing _____" • "The poetry of _____, the writings or essays of _____" • "Historical events surrounding _____, _____"
Formative task 2	*Sources*
	• • •
Formative task 3	*Sources*
	• • •

Designers should review this template for alignment and ask the following questions:

• Do my source notes provide valuable information that is relevant to my question?
• Do my source notes equip students with the information they will need for the final demonstration of knowledge?
• What additional sources might be helpful in responding to the organizing question through completion of the final demonstration of knowledge?

In reflecting on these questions, designers should rewrite their source notes as "shopping list" items. The rewrite should shift from describing the content to describing the type of resources, including the format, like so:

- *From:* "Bills proposing monetary reparations payments were first brought to Congress in the 1860s and have continued to be periodically thereafter"
- *To:* "Primary or secondary source on Sherman's Field Order No. 15" and "a timeline on proposals of reparations to Congress"

As designers recast their source notes as shopping list items, they should notice gaps between their authentic question, final demonstration of knowledge, and first-draft source notes. Their notes were not designed to be a comprehensive list of resources students will need. They are only a starting place. Where designers notice gaps, they should begin to fill them by adding to their shopping list. Designers should continue in this process until there are eight to ten items, similar to the following:

- "Excerpt from _____ autobiography, on the topic of _____"
- "Interview with _____, addressing _____"
- "Excerpts and selected works of _____, demonstrating _____"
- "Testimonio from community members speaking to _____"
- "Primary- and secondary-source documents on _____"

These resource descriptions should be formatted such that they could be entered into an internet or library search engine and, with some trial and error (including reorganizing or rewording the description), produce promising leads.

It is advisable to complete the preceding step and not skip directly to looking for sources. Looking for sources before creating a comprehensive shopping list is like going to the grocery store hungry. It requires some discipline to describe and list the sources, including contents and format, to bridge the organizing question and the final demonstration of knowledge. This step will enable designers to know what they are looking for and whether or not they have found it, which is crucial to this difficult work. When designers skip this step and immediately start searching for sources, it's easy to find sources that might work and rework the project to make them work. It's so much better to know what you need so that you know when you've found it.

Shopping for and Modifying Sources

Setting up tools to stay organized is a worthy investment of time. Creating spreadsheets or running notes documents can allow designers to organize multiple options for a shopping list item and take notes on the contents of potential sources. Notes can include alignment of a source to a given question and the treatment a source might need to be useful (modifying the text, creating an excerpt, etc.). I have used spreadsheets like the one shown in table 7.2 to generate multiple options for a shopping list item, making notes for myself so that I can return to those options later to make my final selection.

A brief review of fair use law concerning use of copyrighted materials for educational purposes may be helpful at this time. Often, designers are more conservative than necessary where use of copyrighted materials is concerned. The Copyright Office's 1976 Guidelines for Educational Fair Use protect the use of copyrighted materials for curriculum-based teaching for educational institutions and education nonprofits. Educational institutions include K–12 schools and districts, colleges, and universities. The guidelines also cover nonprofits that offer educational programming for children or youth, even including institutions like hospitals. Examples of what educators can reproduce for educational purposes are poems (at or under 250 words); a complete book chapter, article, or essay (at or under 2,500 words); and a chart, diagram, drawing, or cartoon from a periodical or book. So long as a designer is using 10 percent or less than the entirety of the published work (e.g., one chapter from a ten-chapter book, one article from a periodical with ten or more articles) and the use is noncommercial (i.e., designers do not plan to charge schools or teachers for the use

TABLE 7.2 *Sample temporary notes document*

Shopping list item	Source link	Notes
<Primary- and secondary-source documents on _____ >	*<Link to option 1>*	Some good info but not strongly aligned to the question
	<Link to option 2>	Paragraphs 3–6 are useful—would need to create an excerpt
	<Link to option 3>	

of their curriculum), designers can be confident in using those materials. This includes both digital versions, where students might follow a link to read a resource, and print versions, where teachers might make copies and provide them to students.

Designers may find resources that are well aligned with the learning objectives but are longer than is reasonable for classroom use, or are useful only in part (i.e., only a part of the article speaks to the topic at hand). Designers may also find resources that will require some modification to be useful to their students. In both these cases, creating an original document that presents an excerpt or a modified version of the original document is advised. Properly citing the original document is important, but not difficult.

Where designers want to use a portion of a document (e.g., part of a chapter, part of an essay or article), they will need to cite the following information at the top of their new document: the author, the title of the original publication, the page numbers from which content is excerpted, and the original publisher and date (e.g., "P. Villeneuve, *Chicano Art for Our Millennium*, pp. 56–59, Bilingual Press, 2004"). I often have included a statement like "Excerpt created by Evan Gutierrez for educational purposes." This is important particularly when a designer is presenting a modified version.

Modifications can make accessible and digestible to students a source text that might otherwise be unusable for the designer's target grade level or band. The most common types of modifications are to alter the reading level of a text by summarizing it using simpler terms and shortening lengthy documents.

Often designers are educators familiar with the expectations of students for reading at different grade levels. For designers who are not educators, or are less familiar with features of text complexity, there are often ways they can change a text that will make it a useful resource to students, regardless of the grade level.

When designers are evaluating whether a text will need to be modified or not, a first step might be to use a Lexile level calculator. *Lexile* is a measure that was created by PhD psychometricians A. Jackson Stenner and Malbert Smith (who formed a company called MetaMetrics). It is a very common measure of quantitative factors that determine the reading level of a text. There are online tools that will quickly determine the Lexile level of a given passage. A designer can then consult a Lexile range chart for that Lexile level.

If a text is on the right level for the grade that the designer is writing for, or within the grade-level band (two to three adjacent grade levels—grades 6–8, for example), significant changes may not be necessary. The designer might recommend reading strategies for more challenging texts as guidance for the user of their project.[2] Limited annotations can add value, but significant tinkering is not necessary.

If the text is outside of the grade-level band for the designer's target audience, there are steps the designer can take to make that text accessible. First, the designer should select only the critical passages of the out-of-range text to modify and present. Significantly modifying a text that is longer than five hundred words is quite a chore. The designer should look for a secondary source to support students' understanding of the concept to accompany the modified text as needed. Second, the designer should simplify vocabulary. Replace polysyllabic or uncommonly used words with simpler terms. In some cases, the designer might annotate an uncommon word with a simple definition or synonym (word with the same meaning—see how I did that?). Designers should feel comfortable replacing complex vocabulary with simpler terms, however, as relying on annotation does little to lighten up a dense passage. The third recommendation is to shorten sentences. Long sentences with multiple clauses can be broken up into shorter, standalone sentences.

These recommendations can make an otherwise unusable text accessible to a variety of reading levels while still retaining what was compelling and valuable about the original text. After making these modifications, designers should recheck their passages for Lexile level and follow the instructions for citing an excerpt, including a statement regarding the modifications they made.

TESTIMONIO AS A SOURCE

Students come from homes and communities that are rich with information. They are surrounded by people who may have had firsthand experience with the themes these projects explore. It is useful and valuable to connect students with that information. *Testimonio* are firsthand accounts from people who have experienced a historical or significant event but are unlikely to give a written account. The term and approach come from Latino studies scholars, who would interview and record people who had experiences and perspectives that would inform the historical record.

It is reasonable for a designer to write in testimonio not as an activity but as a source. Students may be responsible for writing their own interview questions, or those could be provided for them. If students can easily find someone who has had the firsthand experience in question, they might conduct interviews on their own. If that experience is somewhat more rare, or the interview would best be conducted as a classroom-based activity, that is also possible.

In either case, students should record testimonio in a format (most likely written) that will allow for them to refer to and cite this as a resource later. Students should be able to reference notes from these testimonio as sources coequal to others. While students have to *do something* in order to access this information, the purpose of testimonio is not to provide an engaging activity but rather to provide students with community-based knowledge in a tangible, codified form. I encourage designers to engage with this practice and make it part of their projects.

Grouping Sources and Developing Formative Tasks

Prior to this step, designers should have populated a shopping list of eight to ten sources that students will need to reference in order to respond to the authentic question for their project. Designers should also have promising leads for the eight to ten sources they described. They may have created excerpts or modified some of those resources for accessibility, though that is not a prerequisite for the next step. The current state of the temporary notes document might look like table 7-3.

This step has two parts: grouping like or complementary resources and developing tasks for students to complete in interacting with those resources. An example of what the project map might look like when this step is complete is shown in table 7.4. This example comes from a project written by Ericka Streeter-Adams and ELA teachers in Jersey City Public

TABLE 7.3 *Updated sample notes document from table 7.2*

Shopping list item	Source link	Notes
1. Excerpt from _____ autobiography, on the topic of _____	<*Link*>	Some good info but not strongly aligned to the question
2. Interview with _____, addressing _____	<*Link*>	
3. Excerpts and selected works of _____, demonstrating _____	<*Link*>	
4. Testimonio from community members speaking to _____		Have drafted interview questions for students' use
5. Commentary on _____ person and their contributions	<*Link*>	Prioritized political and thought leaders—could revisit as needed
6. Literary analysis of _____	<*Link*>	Quite extensive, may need to be excerpted
7. Interviews with contemporary authors on impact of _____	<*Link*>	
8. Book lists for schools in _____ district	<*Link*>	Included two additional districts for comparison

Schools. Ericka is a seasoned educator and has engaged in multiple design cohorts, inspired to do so by her commitment to providing curriculum to her students that centers on the Black experience in literature. She identifies as a Black woman, writer, spouse, and mother of three. Portions of the project presented in this chapter have been modified slightly from the original for illustrative purposes.

GROUPING

There are three recommended approaches to grouping sources. Designers might start by grouping sources by type (literary, historical, or local sources), as students will interact with each type differently. Grouping by type will clarify the kind of task that students will complete after reviewing the sources. If the majority of the sources are similar in type, designers might instead group by time period. A third option is to group by topic or theme. Often as designers begin to group sources, they employ two of these three approaches (for example, time period and topic).

TABLE 7.4 *Ericka's project map with sources and tasks*

Authentic question: What does it take for Black voices to be heard?	
Theme	*Students will know*
Artistic innovation in Black communities both might face criticism and have lasting impacts. The struggles that Black authors have faced to have their voices heard persist today.	Writing of notable Black women authors, their literary innovations, lasting impacts of their work. Great Black authors have faced challenges to be published—even now, book lists do not reflect communities.

Note on epistemology:

Demonstration of knowledge: Review the school/community demographics (considering gender, ethnicity, etc.), as well as the curriculum reading lists from different subject areas, considering whose voices are present (e.g., immigration stories, Latinx, Black women authors, etc.). Assess the extent to which your community is represented or absent within your curriculum reading list. Create a proposal about changes needed in order to reflect the voices of their communities to be legitimately added to the curriculum reading lists (immigration stories, Latinx, black women authors, etc.). Take action by sharing your proposal with teachers and administrators.

Formative task 1	*Sources*
Students will create a timeline of events for X author, including important events in their early life, publications/professional milestones, and accolades or lasting impact.	• Excerpt from Zora Neale Hurston's autobiography, on the topic of challenges in publishing • Interview with Zora Neale Hurston, addressing criticism she faced • Commentary on Zora Neale Hurston and her contributions

Formative task 2	*Sources*
Students will analyze selected works and provide commentary on X literary devices they used and ways their work was pioneering, citing relevant evidence	• Excerpts and selected works of Hurston, demonstrating her use of Black vernacular • Literary analysis of *Moses, Man of the Mountain* • Interviews with contemporary authors on the impact of Hurston's use of Black vernacular

Formative task 3	*Sources*
Students will write a short argumentative essay on the importance of representation in K–12 book lists, citing both testimonio from community members and published book lists for their district.	• Testimonio from community members speaking to representation in literature used in schools • Book lists for schools in your district

Some sources might not neatly fit into a group. Adding that source to a group and designating it as "optional" is fine in this case. As designers sketch tasks and check for alignment, they might find these resources to be useful after all.

SKETCHING TASKS

Formative tasks should draw only on the information presented in the sources for each group. The tasks should build toward the skills that students will need to respond to the organizing question in the final demonstration of knowledge. The tasks should be ordered from least to most complex.

An example from previous work is a project on the Black and Latinx perspective on gun laws. The organizing question was, "Should gun laws protect rights or people?" The final demonstration of knowledge asked students to make an argument drawing on data relevant to their community, an understanding of the legal dynamics, and the real impacts on people's lives.

- The first task presented data on gun violence and accidental shooting for different populations, asking students to make a claim about what populations are most impacted.
- The second task presented two different perspectives on right interpretations of the Second Amendment, asking students to argue for one of those interpretations while acknowledging opposing viewpoints.
- The third task presented examples of ways people in the Black and Latinx community were impacted by gun violence and how they were responding, asking students to do comparative analyses on the conditions, responses, and outcomes.

The three tasks drew only on the information presented. They also isolated the components of the final demonstration of knowledge. The sequence of the tasks increased in depth-of-knowledge (DOK) level; task 1 is DOK 2, task 2 is DOK 3, and task 3 is DOK 4.[3] Tasks need not increase in DOK level exactly as articulated in this example, but they should not begin with complex or extended reasoning.

Examples from the Design Cohort

Malika

Malika designed a final demonstration of knowledge that would draw on both historical and contemporary examples of Eritrean leaders, and particularly their responses to vulnerable populations. Her project also required some comparison between the Eritrean/Ethiopian model for leadership that she chose to present and other models for leadership.

Her resource shopping list included historical accounts of King Ashama's actions toward the first Muslim immigrants to his country, as well as examples of his rhetoric surrounding those issues. For a contemporary example, Dr. Ralph recommended Nipsey Hussle, a hip-hop artist and community leader with Eritrean roots. Malika hoped to find interviews that would reveal his attitudes about a community's responsibilities to immigrants and disenfranchised peoples.

In order to present contrasting models of leadership, Malika chose to present rhetoric and actions from US President Donald Trump shortly after his election and UK politician (now Prime Minister) Boris Johnson on the topic of Brexit. She hoped to find examples of those leaders making arguments that belied different beliefs about leadership and a leader's obligations to their community.

Malika chose to group these sources by time period. The historical examples referring to King Ashama would be presented first. When designing tasks, Malika decided to separate sources that presented King Ashama's rhetoric from accounts of his actions and their impacts. She decided that designing a single task that referred to both sets of resources would be too complex for the beginning of her project. In the first task, students were asked to make claims about King Ashama's rhetoric and what it suggested about his leadership. In the second task, students were asked to make claims about the impacts that his actions had on immigrants.

Malika chose to group resources that would present rhetoric from both Trump and Johnson. The task that she designed would ask students to make claims about the two leaders' model of leadership, and how that model was revealed by their statements about immigrants.

The final group of resources would present Nipsey Hussle as a modern leader patterned on King Ashama's example. The task would require students to make connections between Nipsey Hussle's rhetoric and Kind Ashama's, as well as contrast Hussle's beliefs about leadership with those of Trump and Johnson.

Malika had difficulty finding resources that presented King Ashama from an Eritrean/Ethiopian perspective. Her supporter, Dr. Ralph, suggested that he might be able to translate some documents for her. Even then, finding a resource that spoke to "indigenous community deliberations" (as Dr. Ralph had described them) proved difficult. With that theme being an anchor for her project, moving forward without such a source was not an option. Malika chose to interview Dr. Ralph on the topic of indigenous community deliberation and cite him as an expert. This allowed her to tailor the interview to surface exactly the themes that students would need and produce a document that was accessible to her audience.

Malika's project map is shown in table 7.5.

TABLE 7.5 *Malika's project map with sources and tasks*

Authentic question: What does the way a nation treat immigrants say about its leaders?	
Theme	*Students will know*
Eritreans/Ethiopians have care for others as a key value relating to leadership, as distinct from some Western models of leadership.	King Ashama and his leadership inform Eritrean cultural values including care for immigrants; various communities have distinct methods for decision-making.
Note on epistemology: Indigenous community deliberations consider many sides of an issue and guide community members to values-based, pragmatic decisions using both mediation and pastoral care.	
Demonstration of knowledge: Students will prepare talking points to inform a response to questions from community members at a town hall regarding the treatment of immigrant communities in their city. Students will gather data on challenges faced by immigrant communities in their city in preparation. Students will represent their values and ways those values inform their position as leaders, specifically their position on care for immigrant communities.	

Formative task 1	Sources
Analyze speeches and documents detailing local indigenous deliberations to determine King Ashama's beliefs and values about refugee communities. Cite evidence and make claims about what his leadership says about his values.	• Description of King Ashama's actions/welcoming of Muslim refugees • Primary and secondary documents that illustrate King Ashama's beliefs and values regarding refugees and his community (value of "pastoral care") • Definitional resource on local indigenous deliberation

Formative task 2	Sources
Analyze primary and secondary documents and cite evidence where King Ashama is making claims about social value and economic benefit, and make claims about the impact of his leadership in these areas.	• Primary and secondary documents describing King Ashama's beliefs about the social values of Muslim refugees and the social impact this had • Description of the political and economic impacts of King Ashama's actions on the region

Formative task 3	Sources
Analyze primary and secondary documents including speeches, press conferences, and town hall meeting documents from and about Boris Johnson and Donald Trump to determine beliefs and values about refugee communities and explain the impact on their communities. Analyze economic and values-based claims for either Trump or Johnson and outline talking points for both.	• Primary and secondary documents describing Boris Johnson's beliefs about the social value and economic risk associated with refugee communities in Great Britain • Impact of Boris Johnson's policies on refugee communities • Primary and secondary documents describing Donald Trump's beliefs about the social value and economic risk associated with refugee communities (particularly those affected by travel bans) in the US • Impact of Donald Trump's policies on refugee communities • Document detailing how to write talking points

Formative task 4	Sources
Analyze primary and secondary documents from and about Nipsey Hussle to identify the role of nongovernmental/community-driven leadership to support refugee communities. What might Nipsey's talking points have been? Cite evidence from sources.	• Context around South Central LA and the needs of the community not being met by governmental entities • Description of Nipsey Hussle's background as the son of an Eritrean refugee • Primary and secondary sources describing Nipsey Hussle's beliefs, values, and actions related to community development and service in South Central LA (value of "pastoral care" should align with SQ1 Source B) • Description of the impacts of Nipsey Hussle's work in South Central LA

Cam

Cam designed a final demonstration of knowledge where students would review their school or district's statements about inclusion and evaluate whether it was sufficient or not. Where it was sufficient, students would create a schoolwide campaign to ensure their peers understood and applied the policy. Where it was not sufficient, students would propose changes to the language.

This demonstration of knowledge provides a local opportunity for students to interact with the relationship between social reality and rules, presenting the possibility both that their rules are advancing social equality but that social reality (understanding and interpretation of those laws) has not caught up, and that the social reality (in this case, the students' own values around inclusion) requires a change to the rules.

Cam knew that students would need to build background knowledge on how laws are made, how they are officially changed, examples of social reasons for change, and times people have challenged and changed laws.

For this purpose, Cam chose to group his sources thematically. His target audience being late-elementary-school students, the link between these thematic groupings would need to be clear. Cam chose to sequence groups of sources, first addressing groups who have fought for social change, some that would be familiar to students and others less so. He followed this by introducing the lenses students would use in this inquiry, specifically "legal equality" and "social reality." Students will then investigate instances when laws changed social reality. Lastly, students would investigate instances when social reality changed laws.

Cam's project map is shown in table 7.6.

TABLE 7.6 *Cam's project map with sources and tasks*

Authentic question: What makes "equality" equal?	
Theme	*Students will know*
Social realities inform laws relating to equality, and vice versa	Landmark cases and civil rights actions establishing equality in relationships; social realities surrounding putting those actions in context

Note on epistemology: Policy documents and discourse around them

Demonstration of knowledge: Students will review class, school, or district rules on inclusion. Students will draft a new or revised policy to propose, or if rules are adequate, create a schoolwide campaign to help other students better understand the policy.

Formative task 1	*Sources*
Complete a graphic organizer that identifies groups who fought for social equality, their reasoning, and successful laws related to their civil rights.	• Video on civil rights movements • Description of the Civil Rights Act (1964) • Description of Nineteenth Amendment (1920) • Description of *Obergefell v. Hodges* (2015)

Formative task 2	*Sources*
Create an infographic defining the terms "legal equality" and "social reality."	• A source describing legal equality and social reality • US Constitution • Video describing how laws are created legislatively and judicially • A list of evidence sources for social reality (opinion polls, media visibility, leadership visibility, hate crime statistics)

Formative task 3	*Sources*
Write a paragraph with examples from three rights movements describing how laws can change attitudes and behaviors.	• A source describing law as a force for social change • A source providing evidence for law shifting behavior related to race • Evidence for law shifting behavior related to gender • Evidence for law shifting behavior related to sexual orientation

Formative task 4	*Sources*
Working collaboratively in small groups, construct a series of claims using evidence about how attitudes and behaviors change laws.	• A source describing how law is based upon social attitudes and behaviors • A source providing evidence for social attitudes shifting law related to race • A source providing evidence for social attitudes shifting law related to gender • A source providing evidence for social attitudes shifting law related to sexual orientation

David

David designed a demonstration of knowledge that would ask students to represent ways either social activism or arts have helped communities process generational trauma. Because that theme anchored on an idea he believed could be unfamiliar to students and teachers (generational trauma), he determined that it would need to be introduced in the resources and described explicitly. David chose to group a resource describing generational trauma with other definitional resources: one describing marginalized communities and another describing social transference (ways trauma is passed between generations).

David also decided to group a set of resources to address root causes (historical events) for generational trauma. These would be followed by resources responding to generational trauma through arts, and separately activists' responses. This thematic grouping would allow for students to build an understanding of key concepts, make connections to root causes, and then examine how communities process traumas through arts and action.

In conversation about finding the right sources for these groupings, I recommended that David consider interviewing his scholar, as the definitional articles on generational trauma were proving hard to find. This presented an opportunity. David's project was being written during a time when policing and police reform were constantly in the news cycle. This seemed to be a logical focus for the project, as students and teachers would likely be thinking about the topic and sources would be easier to find. Issues around policing would work with the arc of the project. They could be explored historically (root causes), seen in artists' work, and addressed by community action. However, in order for the content (in this case, police reform) to eclipse the theme (ways communities process generational trauma), there would need to be another, parallel and unrelated example. It would be necessary to present unjust policing alongside another issue that could be examined in a similar way (historical root cause, multiple examples of community responses). David chose employment as the second social issue to present.

With two social issues in mind, my recommendation to David was to identify examples of ways artists and social activists help their communities process those traumas as a first step. Then, with sources that present those cases clearly and crisply, he would find resources that describe the root causes of those social issues as a second step. The final step would be to pull those threads (the social issues presented for analysis) into the interview questions for David's scholar.

This approach to grouping and the sequencing of tasks for sourcing allows for two prominent, clear examples to be explored in the definitional sources, historical/root cause sources, and the sources around responses or processing. The clarity and consistency of the way the social issues are presented allow for a sharper focus on the theme. The intentionality behind the sequencing of the selection of sources allowed for the most flexibility where the sourcing would be the hardest (using an interview as the definitional piece, starting with selecting sources describing responses).

David's project map is shown in table 7.7.

TABLE 7.7 *David's project map with sources and tasks*

Authentic question: How can communities respond to generational trauma?	
Theme Traumas can be accumulated and passed down within communities, and communities have ways of responding that address both effects and causes of trauma.	*Students will know* The science behind generational trauma and accumulated fear; social justice movements past and present; prominent artists' depictions of traumas and ways communities benefit from these works
Note on epistemology: Shareable social media, web content particular to youth and other social movements in Black and Latinx communities	
Demonstration of knowledge: Students will produce a podcast, article-as-list, or opinion piece outlining important social justice movements, social justice activists, or artists with social purpose. A subset of those profiled will come from students' local communities. Students will use these profiles as evidence to support their response to the question, "How can communities respond to generational trauma?" Students will share their position and perspective, informed by their experiences and community life.	

Formative task 1	*Sources*
Write a paragraph that describes generational trauma, including root causes, ways trauma can be transferred generationally, and effects of generational trauma on Black marginalized communities.	• High-level description of generational trauma. Could center on Black communities, but could include others. (Interview with scholar.) • A definitional resource describing marginalization. • Description of the ways trauma can be transferred from one generation to the next; can include genetic and social transfer.

Formative task 2	*Sources*
Using the provided template, create an outline that compares events from three different time periods that were the result of social injustices aimed at the Black community and the effects they had on society.	• Source describing root causes and historical examples of inequities around employment for Black and brown communities • Sources describing the root causes and historical examples of unjust policing of Black and Brown communities

Formative task 3	*Sources*
Write a review of an artistic work that represents the artist's perspective on accumulated fear and generational trauma in the Black community, citing both works and interviews.	• Interview with artist; article discussing arts as a way for communities to process generational trauma • Artists' response to inequitable employment opportunity • Artists' response to unjust policing

Formative task 4	*Sources*
Write an evidence-based claim about how current social justice movements are addressing causes of trauma to Black and brown marginalized communities.	• Source addressing activism as a community response to generational trauma • Profile of an activist addressing police brutality • Profile of an activist addressing economic oppression

Annabeth

Annabeth designed a final demonstration of knowledge that asked students to evaluate the controversies around reparations in contemporary political debate. To prepare students for this task, Annabeth wanted to familiarize students with the history around reparations, including the injustices that make them necessary, ways different governments and organizations have made reparations, contemporary arguments for or against reparations, and public sentiment around the issue.

Annabeth chose to group sources addressing the preceding points by theme. The first group of sources describes the injustices that establish a need for reparations, focusing mostly on events following the abolition of slavery. Annabeth thought this project presented a unique opportunity for students to learn about exploitation of Black labor post-slavery, Jim Crow laws, and other oppressive actions like poll taxes. The second group of sources would present historical and contemporary examples of governments and organizations making progress toward reparations, including historical examples (such as Sherman's Field Order No. 15) and contemporary examples (such as Georgetown University voting to fund the education of descendants of those that built the campus).

Presenting contemporary arguments for and against reparations required some finesse. The first set of resources selected presented contemporary Black thinkers' arguments for reparations and a White economist's argument against. The White economist's perspective was somewhat pejorative, not only positing arguments against reparations but also suggesting that the arguments for reparations were a little ridiculous. In conversation with Annabeth, we returned to the design principle that all of the sources should represent a perspective that is authentic to the community she was writing for. Annabeth wanted to design a project centered on the Black experience, and determined that this particular source would decenter and marginalize. We looked together for a source that would present an authentic, Black perspective arguing against some forms of reparations. We discovered an interview by Ta-Nehisi Coates with then President Barack Obama, in which Obama suggested that other forms of economic justice would be more effective and less politically costly than reparation payments. This perspective surfaced real tension, worthy of debate among Black leaders, historians, and scholars. By replacing the original resource with the Coates–Obama interview, students would be provided only with sources that reflected perspectives authentic to the community of focus.

The final group of sources presented results of a survey on reparations from both the general public and Black Americans. Both sources being Gallup polls, students would be able to cite statistics that reflected the dominant view, but not narratives that would bully or marginalize.

Annabeth's project map is shown in table 7.8.

TABLE 7.8 *Annabeth's project map with sources and tasks*

Authentic question: Why are reparations so controversial?	
Theme	*Students will know*
The US economy was disproportionately benefited by and under- or noncompensating of Black and brown labor. While some organizations have made reparations, larger efforts are hindered by controversy.	Application of laws to disaffect Black peoples (Jim Crow, *John Punch vs. Anthony Johnson*, etc.); economic realities around Black and brown labor; narratives of enslaved peoples; modern movements toward reparations, both successes and failures.

Note on epistemology: *possibly political speech, remains unclear at this stage*

Demonstration of knowledge: Students will construct an argument (e.g., detailed outline, poster, essay) that evaluates the controversies surrounding reparations using specific claims and relevant evidence from historical and contemporary sources, while acknowledging competing views. Students will investigate local, domestic, and global examples of reparations made by governments, education institutes, or other organizations. Students will use this research to add to their response to the question, "Why are reparations controversial?"

Formative task 1	*Sources*
Construct an explanation of the impacts of Black codes and Jim Crow laws on African Americans today.	• Poll tax receipt • Southern Poverty Law Center article • Excerpt from the article "Exploiting black labor after the abolition of slavery" • List of Jim Crow laws from NPS

Formative task 2	*Sources*
Create a list of ways in which a government or organization has paid or could pay reparations to a group or person.	• Sherman's Field Order No. 15 • Belinda's story: "A Formerly Enslaved Woman Successfully Won a Case for Reparations in 1783" • Georgetown University reparations

Formative task 3	*Sources*
Explain the impacts of monetary reparations as well as public apologies and acts like community building.	• John Tateishi interview excerpt • Roy L. Brooks's Atonement Model • Excerpt from *"Better Is Good": Obama on Reparations, Civil Rights, and the Art of the Possible*

Formative task 4	*Sources*
Write a claim supported by evidence considering why the topic of reparations is discussed in the country today.	• Chart: "Americans' Views on Reparations" (Gallup article) • "Reparations and Black Americans Attitudes About Race" (Gallup article)

III

Using Culturally Sustaining Curriculum in Classrooms

CHAPTER 8

Preparing for Instruction

Previous chapters have addressed the major structural components of culturally sustaining humanities units, including developing questions, identifying content and learning objectives, designing final demonstrations of knowledge, selecting sources, and designing tasks. Throughout these processes, designers have been asked to engage in discovery, seek expert support, and understand the ways positionality impacts design choices to ensure that the components of their projects authentically reflect the intellectual tradition of the community they are writing for.

In this chapter, designers will complete the remaining components of their projects. These include choosing skills (articulated by standards) that students will receive feedback on; engaging in a tuning protocol to ensure that skills, resources, and prompts are aligned; and writing descriptions that will build student and teacher conceptual understanding.

Also described in this chapter are instructional practices that designers should consider when preparing to teach projects. These instructional strategies are congruent with and supportive of the pedagogy of the projects. These will prepare designers to teach projects in their own classrooms or to develop lesson plans, including daily classroom activities, as an optional additional step.

Standards and Skills

For most designers, a conversation about standards comes much earlier in the curriculum or instructional design process. Indeed, examining standards at this late stage may be a tough pill for some to swallow. It could give the false impression that rigor is a secondary consideration in this design process, as many use standards to define rigor. This misinterpretation in turn could lead to these projects being characterized as at odds or inconsistent with the principles that guide rigorous academic work. But in fact, creating instructional materials that ask students to do the most challenging academic work possible is at the heart of this design process. Before I offer guidance on using standards to define rigor, it might be helpful for me to explain why standards are introduced at this stage of development.

Standards represent skills that students will need to demonstrate in order to be successful in school, as well as skills they will need in the life they are preparing for outside of school. As discussed in previous chapters, as new sets of standards are developed across disciplines, they trend toward representing two things: the broad sets of skills that students will need to be successful in college, career, and civic life (e.g., critical thinking, building arguments, synthesizing and representing ideas), and the concepts and discipline-specific sets of skills that adults rely on in a given field (economic theory, science and engineering practices, literary analysis, etc.). This movement in the field rightly places skill development as the central task of teaching and learning, and rightly prioritizes the broadly applicable and discipline-specific skills that students will draw on in their future pursuits.

Specific standards represent these skills, practiced at a certain level. That is, standards are useful to articulate what a skill looks like when it is practiced at a specific level along the learning continuum. They are guideposts that articulate a student's progress in their journey to develop a skill up to the level at which it will be useful to them outside of school. They aid teachers in locating a student along that learning continuum, surfacing useful information on what students will need to progress.

In the design process, both the broad sets of skills that students will practice and the discipline-specific conceptual knowledge that students will gain have already been identified. The broad sets of skills are woven into the final demonstration of knowledge. Aligning those skills to standards and defining the appropriate levels of rigor will allow the designer to write prompts that are crisp and clear, as well as clarify the evidence of mastery that teachers will look for in students' work. The conceptual understandings that students will gain relate to the designer's work to imbue projects with authenticity. Just as frameworks for standards suggest that students should engage with economics like economists, and language arts like writers, these projects are designed to support students engaging with community-centered concepts like elders and scholars from that community. The design process is consistent in spirit with various standards frameworks' treatment of conceptual knowledge, asking that students authentically engage with the concepts presented like adult experts in that field. There are some frameworks for standards that can add clarity to the conceptual knowledge students will gain, and others that will not. This depends on the designer's locality, and will require them to be choosy, selecting only concept-oriented standards that will add value.

Designers should begin this process by identifying their source for standards. I recommend starting with identifying a source for the broad sets of skills that are generalizable and applicable across humanities disciplines. Sources for these include the following:

- Common Core reading and writing anchor standards
- C3 Framework indicators (dimensions 3 and 4)
- Cognitive Skills Rubric (an interdisciplinary rubric, developed by SCALE and Summit Learning, aligned to Common Core State Standards, C3, and Next Generation Science Standards)
- Various PBLWorks rubrics (various rubrics organized by skill, both CCSS and non-CCSS resources)

All of these sources are freely available and readily findable by internet search. For those concerned about alignment to local standards, crosswalk documents may be available to help designers understand how a given locality expects a given skill to be demonstrated. Starting with a national framework to decide on standards that align to the skills students will develop in a given project, followed by a crosswalk with local standards, is the recommended sequence. Depending on the nature of a designer's local standards, these can be a frustrating place to start in this design process.

Designers should now add one or two standards to the box on the project map containing the task description. The example in table 8.1, from Ericka Streeter-Adams's project introduced in chapter 7, uses indicators from the C3 Framework, dimensions 3 and 4.

Designers will use the original task description and standard that they selected to create a prompt. This is a student-facing description of the task, and should be provided for both the formative tasks and the final demonstration of knowledge. The prompt should incorporate all attributes of the standard without fundamentally changing the purpose of the original task. Examples, referring to the project map in table 8.1, are as follows:

Formative task 2: Students will analyze selected works and provide commentary on X literary devices they used and ways their work was pioneering, citing relevant evidence.

C3 D4.1.6–8. Construct arguments using claims and evidence from multiple sources, while acknowledging the strengths and limitations of the arguments.

Prompt: Students will construct an argument on the lasting impact of Hurston on her genre. Students will cite claims made by contemporary authors about how Hurston achieved this impact, including literary techniques and themes they addressed. Students will provide examples from the excerpts of Hurston's works (provided), acknowledging the limitations of their argument, including other authors' contributions and contextual factors.

TABLE 8.1 *Ericka's project map aligned with standards*

Authentic question: What does it take for Black voices to be heard?	
Theme	*Students will know*
Artistic innovation in Black communities both might face criticism and have lasting impacts. The struggles that Black authors have faced to have their voices heard persist today.	Writing of notable Black women authors, their literary innovations, lasting impacts of their work. Great Black authors have faced challenges to be published—even now, book lists do not reflect communities.

Note on epistemology:

Demonstration of knowledge: Review the school/community demographics (considering gender, ethnicity, etc.), as well as the curriculum reading lists from different subject areas, considering whose voices are present (e.g., immigration stories, Latinx, Black women authors, etc.). Assess the extent to which your community is represented or absent within your curriculum reading list. Create a proposal about changes needed in order to reflect the voices of their communities to be legitimately added to the curriculum reading lists (immigration stories, Latinx, black women authors, etc.). Take action by sharing your proposal with teachers and administrators.

Formative task 1	*Sources*
Students will create a timeline of events for X author, including important events in their early life, publications/professional milestones, and accolades or lasting impact. C3 D3.3.6–8. Identify evidence that draws information from multiple sources to support claims, noting evidentiary limitations.	• Excerpt from Zora Neale Hurston's autobiography, on the topic of challenges in publishing • Interview with Zora Neale Hurston, addressing criticism she faced • Commentary on Zora Neale Hurston and her contributions

Formative task 2	*Sources*
Students will analyze selected works and provide commentary on X literary devices they used and ways their work was pioneering, citing relevant evidence. C3 D4.1.6–8. Construct arguments using claims and evidence from multiple sources, while acknowledging the strengths and limitations of the arguments.	• Excerpts and selected works of Hurston, demonstrating her use of Black vernacular • Literary analysis of *Moses, Man of the Mountain* • Interviews with contemporary authors on the impact of Hurston's use of Black vernacular

Formative task 3	*Sources*
Students will write a short argumentative essay on the importance of representation in K–12 book lists, citing both testimonio from community members and published book lists for their district. C3 D4.2.6–8. Construct explanations using reasoning, correct sequence, examples, and details with relevant information and data, while acknowledging the strengths and weaknesses of the explanations. C3 D2.Civ.10.6–8. Explain the relevance of personal interests and perspectives, civic virtues, and democratic principles when people address issues and problems in government and civil society.	• Testimonio from community members speaking to representation in literature used in schools • Book lists for schools in your district

A similar approach can be used to integrate discipline-specific standards into student prompts. Dimension 2 (economics, geography, history, civics) C3 indicators and nonanchor Common Core standards (speaking and listening, for example) can add to student prompts by clarifying the disciplinary bent of a task or project.

In my own practice, I tend to select standards representing broad skills and one discipline-specific set of concepts. This is for a very specific reason: it helps school and classroom leaders determine in what classes projects should be used. If a project is built to align to Common Core ELA standards and civics concepts, that project could be used in a language arts class or a civics class. If a project is built to align to C3 indicators, I might use dimension 3 and 4 indicators and dimension 2 indicators for economics. This project could be used in a general social studies classroom to make the course more culturally sustaining, or used to build an economics elective, for example.

Designers may notice a range of standards that could be applicable. With the interdisciplinary nature of these projects, a designer might identify standards from a variety of disciplines at the task and project level. While this is possible, it does not add much value to writing prompts. Tagging all the standards with potential for alignment can end in a laundry list of standards, representing both broad skills and a number of disciplinary concepts. This is a common practice, born out of concern about accountability for coverage of standards. That is *not* a lens that leads to good design decisions. Just like no one can serve two masters, it is very difficult for a prompt to align to more than a few standards.

Here is an example of a draft task rewritten as a prompt aligned to two standards, both C3 indicators, again from Ericka's project in table 8.1:

Formative task 3: Students will write a short argumentative essay on the importance of representation in K–12 book lists, citing both testimonio from community members and published book lists for their district.
C3 D4.2.6–8. **Construct explanations using reasoning, correct sequence, examples, and details with relevant information and data, while acknowledging the strengths and weaknesses of the explanations.**
C3 D2.Civ.10.6–8. **Explain the relevance of personal interests and perspectives, civic virtues, and democratic principles when people address issues and problems in government and civil society.**

Prompt: Students will write an explanatory essay on how community members might increase the diversity of authors and representation in the approved book list for their district. Students will cite testimonio from community members regarding their perspective on representation in literature and history. Students will reference the current state of representation in their district's approved book list. Students will explain the process by which the approved book list is changed, including specific processes, such as petition, elected position, etc.

Using standards to clarify the task, identify the right level of rigor, and build disciplinary concepts changed the task. It did not change the spirit of the task or the original intention, but the end product changed from an argumentative claim to an explanatory text, buttressed by a concept relating to civic participation and deliberation.

The principle that should guide this phase of the design process is that while projects draw on a number of skills, prioritizing a narrow set of skills improves both the design and the potential for quality assessment. The question ought not be "What skills are students practicing?" but rather "What are the most important skills for students to receive feedback on?"

Checking for Alignment and Engaging in a Tuning Protocol

When a designer has identified sources and written student-facing prompts, the next step is to check for alignment. To do this, designers should respond to the prompt themselves, using only the resources that they plan to provide. It can be tempting to skip this step, but the difference between "close enough" and "good" is worth the time. Designers will have been reading and discussing the topics these prompts address long enough that it's easy for them to rely on their own understanding rather than tight alignment between tasks, prompts, and resources. It is better to "measure twice and cut once" in this step.

In a small minority of cases, designers will complete the task outlined in the prompt using only the sources provided and do so successfully. In most cases, however, designers will come up short on the right information, or the prompt as written will ask students to do something that is almost but not quite possible. There are two potential solutions when this (almost inevitably) comes to pass.

The first solution is to rewrite the prompt to more closely resemble the work that the sources lent themselves to. If the designer has high confidence in the quality of the sources and their fit with the project, this may be the best solution. If only one or two facets (a *facet* being a component of the final product, a type of source to be cited; most good prompts name five to eight) need to be rearticulated, this will not require aligning to a different standard or standards. Think of this as "tuning" the prompt. Where tuning is the right approach, designers should rewrite the prompt to reflect what they were able to achieve with the sources provided. If three to five facets of the prompt don't work or would need to be changed, however, the prompt should be rewritten to align to a different standard or standards. Designers should return to their sources for standards and select alternatives to their first choices, ideally with what worked and didn't work in their response to the prompt still fresh in their minds.

If more than half of the facets of the prompt do not work, the second solution is appropriate: find more sources to either add to or replace the original set. Ideally this will not introduce a change to the shopping list item, only the specific resource that was selected. In many cases, one additional resource will round out the information set that students will need to respond to the prompt. Designers should revisit leads on sources that they had previously abandoned as a first step, and engage in a fresh search where necessary.

Working the sources and prompts into alignment is time-consuming work, but it is the difference between serviceable and good projects. This step is crucial when designers are creating materials that they not only intend to use themselves, but also plan to make available to others. The preceding steps should be repeated until the designer is confident in the grouping of sources, the quality of the individual sources, and the alignment of the prompts to the selected standards.

Separately, designers should complete the final demonstration of knowledge, now checking for the arc of the project (grouped sources and accompanying prompts). These are the questions they should ask at this stage:

- Did the final demonstration of knowledge draw on learning from across the arc of the project?
- Did the final demonstration of knowledge require students to find additional information (from their community, for example), leave

room for the students' point of view, and ask students to own their conclusion?

If the answer is yes to both of these questions, the arc of the project (all prompts, including the final demonstration of knowledge) strikes the right balance between coherence and openness. In this case, the designer should feel very proud of the difficult, complex, and important work they've done.

Teacher- and Student-Facing Language

Writing the Overview and Building a Mental Model

A *mental model* is a belief about the way the world works or the way things fit together that helps people understand and solve problems. Large-scale mental models (like expectancy theory or entropy) help people solve complex problems. On a much smaller scale, a person's mental model of a birdhouse (a visual image, a basic understanding of shape and structure) will help them make the minute, step-by-step decisions like whether to use a butt joint or miter joint for the roof. The clearer the mental model, the more quickly people move from trying to understand the problem to taking the steps to solve it.

Through the process of engaging in discovery, researching, identifying a historical theme to explore, and developing tasks, designers have done the requisite work to share a mental model with their users. A well-written overview will help teachers and students alike to develop a mental model of the big learnings at the end of the project and how they will get there. To build a strong mental model that will help both teachers and students as they progress through the project, the overview should speak as clearly as possible to the historico-cultural theme that the project is organized to address. It is not helpful to bury the lede or dress it up with clever language. As with prompt writing, clear overviews build a strong mental model for the user that they will rely on and return to throughout the project.

A well-written overview should include a punchy articulation of the historical theme of the project, a description of the resources that students will consult (and some reference to the epistemology that shows up in those resources), and a description of the final demonstration of knowledge.

The overview is the first and only place that the designer will state the historical theme their project explores. It does not show up in the questions or prompts explicitly. Here, however, the historical theme should be plain as day, and should be the opening line for the overview. Brevity serves clarity here. Consider the following examples:

> *In both literature and history, Black women authors have had significant impacts, employing literary innovation in order to circumvent social challenges in order for their voices to be heard. Their works have influenced future generations of writers and have become integral to the fabric of American literature.*

> *Black women writers' literary innovations have had lasting impacts on American literature. Their innovations both garnered criticism and gained prominence amidst oppression in ways that continue to shape Black writing today.*

Both examples describe the same historical theme, but the second example uses far fewer words to do so. The second example also hits the same three points (Black writers, innovation, lasting impact) twice. This should produce a stronger, clearer understanding of the central theme than the first example.

The overview should also include a high-level description of the types of source material students will interact with, and the rationale for those sources. If there are three source types (e.g., literary excerpts, interviews with authors, K–12 book lists), a sentence could be dedicated to each. The format could read, "Students will read/review _____ in order to understand _____." These sentences can also be succinct, as additional information will be provided throughout the project.

Lastly, the overview should provide a high-level description of the final demonstration of knowledge. This can be very close to the text used later in the project, edited to fit well in the overview.

Describing the Learner's Journey

Short, descriptive passages to accompany grouped resources and prompts are helpful supports as students and teachers move through the project. These will refer back to their mental model for the project on the whole and orient them to the tasks ahead, making connections between the two. As with the overview, clear and concise language will help users make these connections. If it is difficult for designers to describe the connection, it will be difficult for users to make the connections. Designers ought not worry about oversimplifying such that users miss the nuance. The nuances will be uncovered in their review of the resources, classroom discussions, and response to the prompts.

These short passages should also describe the way that these learnings build on one another over the course of the project. Designers can refer to what students have learned previously and how those learnings relate to what they are about to do. Designers can also refer to what students will do with this knowledge next. Each passage should locate the learner on their journey, reminding them of where they have been, where they are now, and where they will go next. The following passage is a description for formative task 3 in Ericka's "What does it take for Black voices to be heard?" unit shown in table 8.1.

> In previous sections students gained an understanding of Zora Neale Hurston's career, her innovation, and lasting impacts on American literature. In this section students will draw on their knowledge of the challenges Hurston and other Black women faced to be published and recognized, and the value that they add to the Black community. Students will gather testimonio from local community members on their own educational experiences and perspective on the value of Black authors. Students will learn about book lists in their school district and how those lists are made, changed, and by whom. Students will write an explanatory text to share their findings. They will also use this information in their final product, a PSA on the history and value of writers of color in public schools.

This description does not duplicate or reiterate the information included in prompts or detail the resources that students will interact with. It serves only to orient the user to their place in the project in the arc of the project or learner's journey.

The emphasis in both overviews and descriptions is on the style and contents; they are not meant to constrain the volume or level of detail. Some designers will find these examples to be too thin for their liking. For those who would like to provide more information in their overview and description, there are two considerations to bear in mind:

- Adding volume should *not* reduce clarity. Designers can add detail and context, but the central focus should pop.

- These elements are *not* meant to guide instruction. Depending on who the designer's users are and expectations in their context, they may write instructional plans to accompany their project.

Instructional Practices That Support the Pedagogy

This section relates to *how* designers might implement the projects they have created. It can be used in two ways. Where the designer will be implementing one or many of these projects in their own classrooms, these ideas might inform their approach. Where designers intend to write daily instructional plans or implementation guides to accompany their projects, these ideas might be woven throughout those plans.

In either case, it is important to touch on these topics. While this book is not about instructional practice, there are many practices that are congruent with and counter to the pedagogies that have guided the design. What is covered in this section is a short and selective but prioritized list.

Resist Giving Heavy-Handed Feedback

The previous discussion of standards selection points to a philosophy of assessment where both designers and teachers must consider what skills are the most important to be assessed and at what time. Framed with the student at the center, the question becomes "What is the most important feedback for students to receive on their work, and when?"

Teachers should ask themselves this question when considering the relative priority of offering students feedback on grammar and use of "conventions of standard English." Given all of the effort and attention designers have paid to setting students up to demonstrate their knowledge in a way that is authentic to the intellectual tradition of their community, heavy-handed feedback on conventions of standard English would be the wrong feedback to give.

In 1974 the Conference on College Composition and Communication (CCCC) adopted a statement affirming students' right to "their own patterns and varieties of language—the dialects of their nurture or whatever dialects in which they their own identity and style."[1] In the resolution they adopted, the CCCC included this reflection: "We need to ask ourselves whether the rejection of students who do not adopt the dialect most familiar to us is based on any real merit in our dialect or whether we are actually rejecting the students themselves, rejecting them because of their racial, social, and cultural origins."

While most would agree that the resolution is a philosophical and not an administrative document, and many teachers of writing and composition at the college level do not adhere to its edicts, there is merit in its philosophy. What primary and secondary educators might consider is why the CCCC might take such a stance (and reaffirm it in 2003 and 2014). And if primary and secondary teachers understand this position, what might that mean for their work?

A sad truth that relates to these questions is that, when compared to White students, Black and Latino students receive disproportionately more feedback on grammar and conventions of standard English than on their ideas or arguments. Even where White students present opportunities for feedback on conventions of standard English, teachers are more inclined to give them feedback on other skills. Non-White students get "the red pen," while others are coached on developing their ideas.

Teachers have deeply learned that what they should prioritize for student feedback is based, in part at least, on the student's racial, cultural, or ethnic identity. This is a good justification for designers to be clear about what teachers should prioritize in the projects they have designed. Students will receive sufficient feedback on their grammar and use of conventions of standard English in the course of their schooling.

Destigmatize Positionality

A person's race, gender, and class inform their worldview and the meaning-making that they do in academic and nonacademic spaces. It is powerful when instructors model talking about positionality in constructive ways. Particularly White middle-class adults are taught *not* to talk about positionality. In *Culturally Responsive Teaching*, Geneva Gay describes a classroom ritual in which she asks students to declare their racial identity and provide evidence, in part so that her students (largely preservice teachers) know that they will live through it.[2]

Teachers modeling and normalizing discussions about positionality—namely their identity and ways it informs their meaning-making—is important for two reasons. First, it allows teachers to name that they may not have deep knowledge of the intellectual tradition that is being studied and decenters them as the source of truth. Second, and relatedly, it allows them to acknowledge that students may have life experiences and cultural assets that could be uniquely useful in the learning process.

When I work with designers I model that discussions about positionality are meant to be useful, not confessional. The logic that is modeled is "I am ___ and so I have been taught to think in ___ ways." For example:

> I am Evan Gutierrez. I identify as a White and bicultural person. My immediate family is of mixed ethnicity and our cultural practices and traditions include Scots-Irish American, Appalachian, and Mexican American. So in my house we eat biscuits and gravy *and* celebrate Dia de los Muertos. Biculturalism is an important lens for me because it has made me a curious investigator of culture, both in home and in my work.
>
> As a White and bicultural person I have certain assets that I bring to design work. There are also things people perceive I might know which I don't. I am Spanish/English bilingual and speak both languages at home. I'm fluent with certain historico-cultural themes thanks to my life experience and study. I also have no experience of personal racial discrimination, and no familial connection to the immigrant experience.
>
> I grew up poor, around educated and wise people. My personal experience of poverty and access to learned people allowed me to navigate systems of education with knowledge of ways that those systems marginalize the poor. That continues to inform my work, which has been organized around redesigning systems to allow Latinx students to leverage their full set of linguistic and cultural assets in schools.

This narrative names identity markers, identifies perspective or assets that they lend, and also acknowledges certain limitations. It is not sensitive in nature and is not difficult to share (not confessional). More importantly, it relates directly to the work at hand (meant to be useful). If teachers are prompted to model this behavior for students, they should highlight that this is not disclosure for its own sake. It is intended to set students up to be thoughtful about the ways that their identities and experiences can contribute to their learning and to their biases, and about the fact that those around them may have different perspectives based on their positionality.

Do prompt teachers to enter into this practice with authenticity, naming the most true and relevant experiences for the learning at hand. If there is not a clear connection, statements like "Based on my values, I care about diverse narratives and histories being part of what we discuss in class, even when those narratives are not familiar to me" are better than stretching to make an obtuse connection. Students will pattern their behavior on whatever is modeled. If contrived or confessional statements are what's modeled, students will follow suit.

Don't create an expectation that students will reciprocate. Teachers should plan on modeling this behavior multiple times before seeing it show up in student discourse, if that happens at all. Making statements about the learners' positionality should not be standardized as an activity. There is a reason that this is not part of the curriculum design—the goal is to normalize talking about positionality, not to codify it.

Facilitate Productive Classroom Discourse

Where designers plan to either teach these projects themselves or create daily lesson plans to be used by others, it is important to keep in mind the goal of a dialogue-rich classroom. The project itself is designed around a small number of carefully crafted questions. In the teacher's daily instruction, there will be dozens more. These are intended to check for understanding, guide students through the learning process, and ultimately build a dialogically rich and responsive environment. The north star is for the dialogue to be authentic, a real exchange of ideas between and among students and their teacher. Those with classroom experience know how difficult and elusive that state can be at times.

A sequence of discussion questions might begin with questions that the teacher knows the answer to, but the questioning should not stay there. When all questions are answerable by the teacher, they have produced "pseudo-discourse."[3] A sequence of questions may start with such questions but should lead to questions where there is an interpretive lens or perspective at issue. Questions requiring recall or recitation (What happened?) should lead to open questions (How do things like this happen? What might happen next?). Teachers should prepare questions that start shallow but lead the discourse into deep and open waters.

Some of what students will contribute might be anticipated, and some will not. Teachers should prepare for students to posit ideas, perspectives, and questions that are unique. These contributions will change the classroom discourse and potentially other aspects of instruction. Particularly where a teacher does not have the privilege of familiarity with the topic, it is important that they embrace and not redirect unanticipated responses.

When teachers have guided students into those deep open waters of authentic discourse, they may need some tools to keep the conversation productive while resisting the very natural urge to control it. Here are some generalizable techniques that teachers might lean on as they navigate open discourse on new content:

- *Acknowledge unique perspectives:* "Thank you for sharing that perspective. I have not had that experience, but I can see how that relates, so I'm glad I have the opportunity to learn about it."
- *Make connections:* "Thank you for this contribution. What you shared makes me think of _____ that we read. Is that the right connection to make, or are there other things you would highlight as a connection?"
- *Make invitations:* "That is an awesome insight that you shared. I wonder if others noticed similar things?"
- *Make adjustments:* "I can see that a lot of us have similar perspectives on this issue. I'll make sure as I'm preparing our next conversations that we revisit this for further discussion."

CHAPTER 9

Sharing the Work

I n this final chapter, designers will consider ways to share their work with their community. How will you describe this work to colleagues? How might you connect with like-minded teachers in your local context and beyond? How will you talk with parents and community members about this approach? Building a community around an idea, particularly a divergent idea, is a crucial component of that idea's prospects for success and longevity. Different stakeholders should be invited into conversation and engagement in a way that speaks to their needs, concerns, and interests. Rather than building buy-in to prevent disruption or quiet criticism, this could be seen as the teacher or school leader developing a network of supporters who will help sustain this transformational work.

Building a Community Around an Idea

In one of the first cohorts of designers that I supported in writing projects using an early version of this design process, a scholar that was supporting the work called out something that he found to be unique. Dr. Héctor García Chávez, who was the director of the Latino Studies program at

Loyola University Chicago, had agreed to meet with the cohort, share perspective on projects, and recommend resources. His observation was that we had "built a community around this idea" that we were working on. He was commenting about the way the designers worked and talked with each other—that when he joined the group for discussion each designer took time to introduce themselves and talk about their connection to the work. He was invited to do the same: rather than enter and lecture, he was invited to talk about himself and his life, which led to discussion of the work and designers' questions about their projects. Dr. García Chávez suggested that we had built a strong core, and that in our schools and communities the circles of inclusion would grow and this ultimately "would be the thing that sustains the work."

His comments point toward a difference in mind-set that this work required when compared to other efforts involving curriculum or program design and rollout. The difference is best described as one between communities and systems. In communities, individuals are unique, have choices, and contribute to the whole. In systems, behavior is shaped by information, structure (like hierarchy), and resources. Dr. García Chávez suggested that this effort had built a community, made up of individuals who had unique personal investments in the work and who would make unique contributions. Many who have worked in K–12 settings will have had personal experiences of the ways systems shape work through information, use of structural authority, and provision or withholding of resources.

Every school system that I have ever worked with was both a community and a system. It is overly simplistic to suggest that school systems might be one or the other, or even that they might skew toward one over the other. What is true, however, is that when designers take their projects out of development and into the world, the way they share that work has implications for how it will be received. My suggestion is that designers build a community around their ideas, which I believe will serve the growth and longevity of those ideas.

Invitation Versus Buy-in

I have been party to countless conversations with teachers and administrators about rolling out new and exciting initiatives, and some not-so-exciting ones. A key element of these conversations is buy-in. Some educators have believed that the success or failure of our efforts would come down to one thing: buy-in. How to generate it, whether or not we got it—decision-makers would wring their hands over or hang their hats on buy-in. It is important to acknowledge that the idea of buy-in in school contexts is an evolutionary step forward from a time when administrators relied solely on positional authority. Nonetheless, as a person with (among others) a degree in business, when I am part of conversations about buy-in I ultimately hear crude underlying questions: Did you get your stakeholders on board? Did you successfully sell the idea, and did they buy it?

The problem with this question is that it is binary: the answer is either yes or no. When implementing new initiatives I would often be asked whether or not I got the principals' buy-in, or if I had the right teachers bought in. The honest answer was never binary. It always included shades of yes that spoke to the individual's needs, priorities, or concerns.

Invitation is a different frame for conversation about a new idea and the change that it may bring. Unlike buy-in, an invitation is nontransactional. It asks a person in, rather than asking for a person's resources in a sales-like exchange. When a person is invited in, they will bring their perspective, priorities, and concerns. They will be invited to make unique contributions. These considerations suggest that they might not only receive "the thing," but also *change* "the thing."

A person may be invited in and disagree for a period of time. Their concerns may not be resolved right away, but because they are in relationship, they may come around. "This is what we're doing; this is why it's great. Are you in?" asks for stakeholder buy-in in a way that requires a yes or no. When someone has been presented with a choice about something new and said no, they are unlikely to reverse that answer at any point in the future. In contrast, asking, "This is what we're thinking about; what is your perspective? Do you think you might help with this part?" or "How would this work in your classroom or school?" presents different entry points into a sustained effort. A person is asked to bring their experience, ideas, and maybe even help. The invitee is never "on or off the bus." When speaking about this work with colleagues, I have sometimes presented a number of ways to engage, the least involved being to "stay informed as the work develops." Some colleagues who chose this option early on are now among the most powerful and fervent supporters of the work.

Elements of the systems approach to change will enter the picture. Ideally there will be information sharing among leaders, the support of people with positional authority, and resources allocated to these efforts. Still, designers should work to build a community around their ideas, if for no other reason than that it will sustain them. When designers look around them and see "thumbs up" or "thumbs down" to their work, it is easy to become disheartened. When they see people who may help in big and small ways, whether those invitees are in love with or confused about the idea itself, they are sustained by community.

Elements of Invitation

There are certain characteristics of an attractive invitation, whether extended to parents, colleagues, or students. The ways different community members' needs will be cared for in the invitation are described in the latter half of this chapter. Different people will have unique concerns, interests, and resources they might bring to bear. No matter the invitee, however, a good invitation into community will have the following elements in common.

PERSONAL INVESTMENT

Think about a time someone shared something they were excited about with you. Think about the enthusiasm that they expressed, statements about what changed for them, and their emotional involvement. Now think about the response that it evoked in you—maybe you experienced some of the same emotions, even if to a lesser degree. Excitement, interest, or happiness may have stirred in you as you were listening to their account. It is normal for us to mirror the emotions our neighbors or colleagues express when they share something that is important to them. Beginning an invitation by sharing your personal investment creates an opportunity for *positive empathy*, what researchers define as "understanding and vicariously sharing others' positive emotions. Imagining, recalling, observing, or learning of others' positive outcomes can trigger positive empathy."[1]

Our intuition may lead us to start these conversations with statements about "why this work is important" and cite theory or statistics that support our position, which tends to get listeners' critical thinking wheels turning. Starting a conversation instead with "why this work is important *to me*" has an entirely different effect. The listener will then look for points of connection like shared experiences or values and other ways to empathize. This is an invitation into a relationship, or to deepen an existing relationship, which reinforces the long-term goal of building a community around this work.

CURRENT STATUS

A short accounting of what has already taken place, what is currently in process, and what you hope will come allows for the invitee to feel (and be) read in on your work. This creates a sense of collegiality, suggesting that the listener is capable of grasping the full scope of this work. This levels the field of engagement, bringing people up or down a rung on the hierarchical ladder toward the center, closer to you. This engenders the sense that all are colleagues in this work.

This approach runs counter to the experiences that many have had of the systematized power imbalances in K–12 schooling and their effects on trust between those in different roles.[2] Teachers have significantly more power than students and parents, school leaders have more power than teachers, administrators have dramatically more power than school leaders, and so on. Engaging all invitees with the expectation that they should grasp the full arc of this work, that they are privy to the same information (even if presented differently), is a powerful posture to take.

REQUESTS FOR SUPPORT

Requests for support can take many different forms, depending on the invitee and the various stages of the work. Whether for perspective, at-home support, in-school collaboration, or systems-level advocacy, requests for support turn listeners into collaborators. Soliciting the invitee's aid gives them an opportunity to invest and hence take some ownership of the work. Even the most reluctant supporters are often willing to respond to a request for help. The request for and granting of help is an example of an exchange of social capital, which boosts morale in a community even more predictably than indicators of social capital like network strength or organizational participation.[3] Individual solicitation of support, even when the tasks are small, will lead to a happier and more connected community of supporters than some traditional methods for organizational change.

Offering a variety of opportunities to invest, from light and in-the-moment ("What are your thoughts on this?" or "How would this work in your context?") to more substantive investments, also puts the invitee in control of the contribution they would like to make. A designer who has produced a few projects could approach a colleague and ask, "Would you like to pilot one of these projects in your classroom and offer feedback? If that's not feasible right now, would you consider reading through one and sharing your thoughts?" The invitee who declines to pilot but agrees to read and offer feedback is more likely to pilot later. This is not a manipulation, but rather an acknowledgment that the invitee knows their own resources, and asks "What is the right level of investment for you, *at this time?*" recognizing that their level of investment might change later.

How to Invite

The preceding elements are not ordered. There is not a formula for invitation into community. These invitations and reinvitations will take many forms. These invitations can be issued to students before and during projects, to parents during conferences and in emails, with school leaders to establish a design cohort, or to school boards to approve electives. My urging would be to notice, in practicing offering invitations, which elements come easily and which are difficult. This will help and inform preparation, because questions will come and concerns will be raised. The work of centering nondominant narratives so that all students have the opportunity to see their community as worthy of study presents a change, and conflict is inherent to change.

If one notices that personal investment and current status come easily but requests for support do not, it is wise to invest time in drafting some examples pertaining to situations that may come up.

Example of invitations to a parent:

"I know that this is different from what your student is studying in other classes, Mr. _____, so it would be so helpful if you would ask him at home about what he's learning, and how he's feeling about it, every so often. Would you do that? Also, your student will be asked to interview a family member about _____ later in the project, so if you're willing to think through who they might talk to, that would be awesome!"

Example of invitations to a colleague:

"You know, Mrs. _____, I know these projects are different from what you're accustomed to teaching. If you could look these over with me, and think about how I can connect this content to what students learned with you, that would be so helpful. I know students would benefit from those connections."

It is good practice to anticipate where questions or concerns might come from, and think through the elements of invitation that might be harder to come up with off the cuff, write them down, and internalize them. It has been my experience that criticism does not always come with a calendar invitation, so I recommend thinking through who might need to be invited and in what way.

Anticipating Criticism and Concern

As stated earlier, when engaging in divergent work, anticipate criticism and concern. Certain themes tend to come up when this work moves from the drawing board to the classroom. Different people may articulate the same fundamental concerns in different ways. One's ability to recognize the concern that is being expressed, even when it's expressed in a variety of ways, and respond in a confidence-inspiring manner will help community members to continue to invest. These recurring themes include rigor, sensitive content, and change aversion.

Rigor

All community members want students to be engaging in challenging academic work. They may have conceptions of what that work should look like that differ from the projects designed in this process. The following statements and questions come from community members who have different roles (administrators, parents, students) but share that sentiment:

- "Your project sounds interesting, but I'm not sure it's going to get anyone into college. Isn't that your job—to get them into college?"

- "We should be focusing on literacy—skills that are going to make a difference for these kids."
- "Is anybody going to need this in the real world? Why prioritize this over American history?"

I have heard all of these, in slightly different forms, from parents, colleagues, and decision-makers. The ideas that I base my responses on have been discussed in previous chapters and will be familiar to designers. They are presented differently based on the background knowledge of the community member. Parents deserve care and consideration in these conversations, as practices have shifted significantly since many of them were students themselves. With colleagues, one can assume a shared vocabulary and baseline understanding of the principles that drive this work.

Responses to concerns about rigor should touch on two key points. This first is that standards articulate the skills that students should practice, up to a standard that is developmentally appropriate. These projects have been built with keen attention to the skills that students will need both in school and life outside of school. The second point is that students are able to do more challenging academic work when they are engaged and invested in the learning process. When a student has background knowledge to bring to bear, they can practice the skills the project is fostering at a higher level, using their cultural capital and community-based knowledge as a lever. Here are some examples of responses to different community members that touch on both points:

- "Thank you for your question, Mr. _____. We are invested in students' prospects for college. Colleges are increasingly looking for skills like reasoning, selecting evidence to build arguments, and writing persuasively. In fact, the tests students take for admission ask students to demonstrate those skills. And because the students are so interested in this topic, they're working hard on those skills."
- "Dr. _____, you know as well as I do that the standards point to skills and not content. You also know, and I see in my school, that engagement is a prerequisite for doing rigorous academic work. Students are taking ownership over this work in impressive ways, and the skills that are identified in these projects are our priority skills."

Both of these responses should be followed by an invitation, with all of the elements. Touching on the role of standards and student engagement will prevent myths and misconceptions from taking hold. The community members themselves are not the myths. Dispel the myths, and reinvite the community members into support and investment.

Content

Many community members' beliefs about school anchor on content, and whether content familiar to them is being taught. Concerns about content may be raised if community members perceive the content to be nontraditional, sensitive, or both. This is a nearly universal dynamic, not true of work around cultural relevance alone. Many reading this text will have been involved in lengthy conversations about "the new math," which is an example of a concern about nontraditional content. Here are examples of concerns raised about content:

- "I think these projects are a fine activity so long as they're not taking time away from the traditional American history."
- "This is mature stuff—why would you think this is appropriate for students? Are teachers prepared to teach this?"
- "I think this is fine for *some* students. But not everyone needs or is going to like this."

There are two key points to touch on when responding to concerns about content. The first is inclusion, which will draw on strategies shared with Cam by Johanna Eager, director of the Welcoming Schools Initiative for the Human Rights Campaign. School-, district-, or even classroom-level value statements often touch on inclusive learning spaces. Responses can bridge these statements to classrooms where students with different backgrounds can see themselves in the curriculum, or learn about the experiences of those who are different from them. The second is that the curriculum is not the content; the curriculum has been thoughtfully crafted to support discourse *about the content* that is developmentally appropriate. Even challenging texts and topics can be discussed productively when the curriculum asks the right questions and presents the right tasks. Example responses include the following:

- "In our school, we strive for all students to be fully included. That means that we learn about different people's perspectives and experiences. The curriculum does not ask that all students come to the same conclusion, but that they engage in productive and respectful dialogue."
- "With our diverse student body, we believe that it is important for all students to see themselves in the curriculum. That means some will strongly identify with the content, and some will be enriched by it. The traditional curriculum has not always done this well. These projects were written in such a way that there is important learning for all students. There is space for those who identify with the content and those who will be learning about communities and experiences that are different from their own."

CHANGE AVERSION

The last set of concerns, change aversion, is slippery and difficult to pin down. It is characterized by a general uneasiness or discomfort. That general uneasiness, by its own nature, is not always articulated clearly. It is sometimes expressed through a salvo of seemingly unrelated concerns, where the only clear through-line is queasiness and discontent. Education is a field of practice that is structured by convention. There have always been innovators, however, and most educators are deeply invested in growing in their practice in order to better serve their students. Even so, many of the facets of life in schools are a function of convention. Accordingly, stakeholders are conditioned to meet challenges to convention with skepticism. Even people who are motivated by innovation in other aspects of life will push back against evolution in school programming.

Statements that point to change aversion in community members' attitudes are characterized by confusion. Sentences will contain the phrase "I don't know why." It is wise to pay attention to these statements. Community members are being honest about their confusion—they don't understand the reasons behind the changes. In some cases they may be referring to a lack of information. In others they may be referring to a mismatch in worldviews. Examples include the following statements:

- "I don't know why there's all this pressure to innovate and change things. All of us were products of this system and we seemed to have turned out all right."
- "Why do you think you can change what our kids are learning?"
- "What's this social experiment all for, anyway?"

There are two key points that responses to change aversion should touch on. The first point is that the system hasn't always worked well for everyone. There is systemic inequity that has real impacts on students' lives and prospects. It is well documented that the curriculum doesn't address the needs of all students, and these deficiencies have real, tangible consequences. The second point is that the world has changed. Cultural competence is a required skill in college and professional life. This means that students who are not equipped to have conversations about cultural differences in productive ways will be at a real disadvantage. Here are two example responses that touch on both key points:

- "I recognize that change is hard, but it's also necessary. Not all students have had their experiences or identities validated in school. This can lead to students feeling invisible, and that has real, lasting impacts. Students who don't face that challenge benefit as well. They will build empathy, which is a skill that will serve them for the rest of their lives."
- "I don't know about you, but I wasn't afforded the chance to learn about the history of people like me in school. It is an uphill battle, but I want to afford my students opportunities that we didn't have. Our work is to prepare students for life outside of school, and building a strong and positive self-concept is an advantage I would like to give them."

All of the sample responses in this section should be accompanied by an invitation, including a personal investment, current status, and request for help. Even when the concerns are not couched in a respectful way, they point to a genuine conflict between the work that's being done and the community member's understanding of what's best for students. This can cause frustration, and in moments of frustration it is very easy to dismiss some community members as people who "just don't get it." In many cases, they don't. Part of the work of community building is recognizing that pieces of criticism point to a gap in understanding between a community member's conception of school and what is being proposed or implemented. They're asking for that gap to be filled. The community members that we invite into the work with us will fall along a spectrum of understanding and readiness to fully embrace it. Gaining information, investing their own efforts, and hearing about ways this work is benefiting others will move people from the outer rings of the circle closer to the core over time.

Examples from the Design Cohort

Annabeth

Annabeth was not able to teach her project in the same academic year she designed it, as the design cohort ran from January to the end of April. She did, however, build her project into a middle school social studies course to be taught in following years, aligned to the new Kentucky state standards. Annabeth also accepted a role as a school administrator over curriculum and instruction in her district. In that new role and in discussing this work with colleagues, Annabeth described her participation in the design cohort as transformational, challenging, and changing her core assumptions about curriculum design. She shared that the early steps of finding a protagonist and discovering the questions they would pose to us today shook up her beliefs about whose stories should be told in the formal curriculum, and if we were asking the right questions about those stories. She has discussed these experiences with her colleagues in efforts to pass these mind-sets on, and to lay the groundwork for her project to be taught well in the coming year.

Annabeth's collaboration with scholars was a particularly impactful part of the process for her. The step of connecting with scholars who have deep familiarity with the community that she was writing for required her to acknowledge that she is not part of that community and needed input in order to do justice to the historical themes she had selected. Meeting and working regularly with Black scholars significantly impacted the arc of her project and ensured that the questions, sources, and tasks were authentic to the stories she wanted to center. Annabeth stated that this step taught her to "listen more than speak" and that this experience was formative as she seeks to support and advance authentic reconciliation in her community.

Cam

Cam discussed his project work with a number of LGBT colleagues. These discussions affirmed the authenticity of his central question as being of inherent importance to the LGBT community. Additionally, colleagues shared appreciation for having a project written for upper elementary students, as there is a dearth of curricula that address issues of gender and sexuality with this age group. The design process strengthened Cam's belief that with the right sources and supports, even young students can tackle complex issues.

Cam's conversations and previous experience reminded him that teachers are often comfortable discussing the civil rights and women's rights movements, but consider gender identity and sexuality "out of bounds" for their classrooms. This has a silencing effect, and actively erases LGBT people from the curriculum. While Cam's project referenced both, he and his colleagues were proud to have the final demonstration of knowledge center on LGBT history. His hope is that LGBT students and those with LGBT parents will be affirmed by seeing their histories represented in a positive light. He also hopes that his project will have a humanizing effect for students who are not LGBT. Cam suggested that when we don't discuss LGBT issues or introduce LGBT people, we can wrongly send the message that they are flawed or shameful, and he hopes that his project will counteract these messages.

The design process built a framework and language for Cam to rely on for future work, particularly around ways that curriculum can be both sustaining and broadening. In the field of culturally relevant and sustaining pedagogy, there is sometimes an unspoken undercurrent that we should broaden representation by matching materials to the communities we serve—for example, ensuring the prominence of materials on the Latino experience in school communities with large Latino student populations. The problem with that "matching" emphasis for LGBT students and the children of LGBT parents is that they are never the majority in any school community, which risks ensuring their experience is never discussed. Cam has therefore come to appreciate the importance of discussing LGBT representation in curricular materials as both *sustaining* for LGBT students and families, and *broadening* for non-LGBT students and families.

David

David will use the project that he wrote and others like it to make humanities courses more relevant and sustaining for the students and teachers that he supports as a building administrator. While he is interested in teachers using the project that he designed, he is also aware of and excited by the growing number of similar projects that are available. David came away from the design cohort experience with language and core understandings that he will need to support teachers integrating culturally sustaining projects into their scope and sequence. He has also begun to extrapolate instructional moves and look-fors that will allow him to support teachers with high-quality implementation. He plans to use these tools and strategies to ensure that students in his school will have regular access to culturally sustaining curriculum and learning spaces.

Malika

Malika is using the project that she wrote and her learning from this design process to elevate the work her organization does around culturally sustaining pedagogy. Where previously, she focused on a culturally sustaining instructional framework that was curriculum-agnostic, she believes that pairing that framework with units and projects written with relevance in mind will improve the educator and student experience. As a designer of both curriculum and professional development, Malika is excited for the materials and the new perspective that her participation in the cohort has yielded. Coaching teachers to implement projects written using this process will allow Malika to build systems of support that have promise to scale.

Malika reported feeling well positioned to support curriculum teams to recognize how culturally sustaining units of inquiry are not supplemental "nice-to-haves." Rather, they have the potential to improve engagement and access to deeper learning and grade-level standards. These projects allow students to understand and experience learning that empowers them to lead meaningful change in their communities. This connection alone should be a key component of our conversations around high-quality curriculum.

Personally, Malika appreciated being able to critically engage with the history of her own people across geography and time. Her family are East African refugees who came to the US with the hopes of establishing a life of peace, safety, and self-determination. She is aware that many immigrant families must negotiate conflicting cultural values and expressions through a deeply personal journey of identity exploration, which develops the multicultural lens necessary to navigate different spaces with both empathy and critical reflection. However, when this process of identity development and cultural navigation happens in spaces that do not honor one's cultural identity, it becomes difficult to engage in those spaces. Malika's personal conviction is that schools must recognize the ways in which they can be sites either of honoring and facilitating identity development or of perpetuating white supremacy. Until college, she herself did not find spaces where she didn't have to separate aspects of her cultural expression in order to engage in critical discourse. This is a problem. Her participation in the cohort instilled a sense of hope that young scholars will have access to spaces that facilitate critical discourse by centering their various identities.

It is with this hope and confidence in the capacity of educators to build this future that I offer this framework for designing culturally sustaining curriculum.

Why Are Reparations Controversial?

Eighth-Grade US History Inquiry

Supporting Questions

1. How did Black codes and Jim Crow laws harm Black people after slavery ended?
2. How have organizations and governments used reparations?
3. What are the potential impacts of reparations?
4. Why are reparations currently being discussed?

Why are reparations controversial?	
C3 Framework indicators	D2.His.14.6–8. Explain multiple causes and effects of events and developments in the past. D4.8.6–8. Apply a range of deliberative and democratic procedures to make decisions and take action in their classrooms and schools, and in out-of-school civic contexts.
Cognitive skills	Informational/explanatory thesis, selecting relevant sources, explanation of evidence, argumentative claim
Staging the compelling question	Generate questions surrounding the concept and forms of reparations.

Supporting question 1	*Supporting question 2*	*Supporting question 3*	*Supporting question 4*
How did Black codes and Jim Crow laws harm Black people after slavery ended?	How have organizations and governments used reparations?	What are the potential impacts of reparations?	Why are reparations currently being discussed?
Formative performance task	*Formative performance task*	*Formative performance task*	*Formative performance task*
Create a mind map demonstrating the different impacts of Black codes and Jim Crow laws on Black people.	Create a list of ways in which a government or organization has paid or could pay reparations to groups or individuals.	Write one or two paragraphs explaining the impacts of reparations in the form of monetary reparations, public apologies, and/or acts of community building.	Write an evidence-based claim considering why reparations are currently being discussed in the country today.
Featured sources	*Featured sources*	*Featured sources*	*Featured sources*
Source A: Artifact, Alabama poll tax receipt Source B: Article, "Voter Suppression" Source C: Article, "Exploiting Black Labor After the Abolition of Slavery" Source D: List of Jim Crow laws	Source A: Article, "Sherman's Field Order #15" Source B: Article, "A Formerly Enslaved Woman Successfully Won a Case for Reparations" Source C: Article, "Georgetown Students . . . Create Reparations Fund"	Source A: Article, "Japanese Americans' Campaign for Reparations" Source B: Op-ed, "Reparations Are an Opportunity . . ." Source C: Interview, Barack Obama	Source A: Gallup survey data, "Americans' Views on Reparations" Source B: Gallup survey data, "Black Americans' Attitudes About Race"

Summative performance task	Argument: Construct an argument (e.g., detailed outline, poster, essay) that evaluates the controversies surrounding reparations using specific claims and relevant evidence from historical and contemporary sources, while acknowledging competing views.
	Extension: To extend their arguments, students can research international examples of reparations (or reparations debates).
Taking informed action	Understand: *Embedded in the inquiry's supporting questions.* Assess: Deliberate on the potential impact of reparations. Act: Create a student guide explaining the situation and reparations, including a list of credible resources for learning more about reparations.

Overview

Inquiry Description

This inquiry leads students through an investigation of the use of reparations to make amends for the enslavement, exploitation, and generational racism Black people have endured. The compelling question, "Why are reparations controversial?" asks students to evaluate the controversy surrounding reparations payments, engage with narratives of Black people, and compare precedents set by organizations and governments. This investigation spans the Antebellum Era through the twenty-first century to highlight the ongoing struggle for equality.

As students move through the inquiry, they are asked to consider the treatment of enslaved people and the echoing effects of systemic oppression. Building from previous learning about the institution of slavery in America, students analyze the impacts of racism on generations of people of color and the legal institutions and systems that continued to take advantage and oppress marginalized groups. Using a range of primary and secondary historical sources, students examine arguments surrounding the practice, as well as the forms that reparations may take. The four supporting questions, the formative performance tasks, and the featured sources are designed to build the students' reasoning as they grapple with the compelling question.

It is important to note that this inquiry requires prerequisite knowledge of the institution of slavery, race-based social hierarchies, the contributions of both free and enslaved Blacks to the culture and infrastructure of the country, and the systems put into place after 1865 that perpetuated a social caste system. If needed, teachers can provide applicable sections from Howard Zinn's *A Young People's History of the United States* and/or Ronald Takaki's *A Different Mirror for Young People.*

Note: This inquiry is expected to take ten to twelve 45-minute class periods. The inquiry time frame could expand if teachers think their students need additional instructional experiences (e.g., supporting questions, formative performance tasks, featured sources, writing). Teachers are encouraged to adapt the inquiry to meet the needs and interests of their students. This inquiry lends itself to differentiation and modeling of historical thinking skills while assisting students in reading the variety of sources.

Structure of the Inquiry

In addressing the compelling question, "Why are reparations controversial?" students work through a series of supporting questions, formative performance tasks, and featured sources in order to construct an argument supported by evidence while acknowledging competing perspectives.

Context of the Inquiry

This inquiry was developed through a collaboration between C3 Teachers and a team of Summit Learning curriculum fellows. This collection of inquiry projects was designed to meet the needs of states and districts, who are increasingly calling for ethnic and gender studies' inclusion in their school curriculums. Schools need culturally relevant materials that represent the histories and experiences of the communities they serve. The focus on culturally relevant curriculum is an inclusive focus. Culture is not a thing that some people have and others do not. This project, and others in the collection, represents a diverse set of identities and perspectives.

Additional Resources

Kattah, M. L. (n.d.). Reparations Debate. *Teaching Tolerance*. Teacher Resources. Accessed from: https://www.tolerance.org/learning-plan /reparations-debate.

- Teachers can find additional sources on reparations from *Teaching Tolerance.*

Matthews, D. (23 May 2014). Six times victims have received reparations—including four in the US. *Vox.* News article. Accessed from: https://www.vox.com/2014/5/23/5741352/six-times-victims-have-received-reparations-including-four-in-the-us.

What Students Are Saying About Reparations, What They Want to Learn in School, and Individuality. (12 December 2019). The Learning Network. *New York Times.* News article (Current Events Conversation). Accessed from: https://www.nytimes.com/2019/12/12/learning/what-students-are-saying-about-reparations-what-they-want-to-learn-in-school-and-individuality.html.

Willis, T. A. (8 September 2019). What Do Reparations Look Like. *Morningside Center for Teaching Social Responsibility.* Teacher Resources. Accessed from: https://www.morningsidecenter.org/teachable-moment/lessons/what-do-reparations-look.

Cognitive Skills

The Summit Learning Cognitive Skills Rubric is an assessment and instruction tool that outlines the continuum of skills that are necessary for college and career readiness. Cognitive skills are interdisciplinary skills that require higher-order thinking and application.

The rubric includes thirty-six skills and eight score levels applicable to students in grades 3 through 12. Through Summit Learning, students practice and develop cognitive skills in every subject and in every grade level. The use of a common analytic rubric for assessment of project-based learning allows for targeted, standards-aligned feedback to students and supports the development of key skills over time. For more information, see the Cognitive Skills Rubric here: https://cdn.summitlearning.org/assets/marketing/Cognitive-Skills-Document-Suite.pdf.

The inquiry highlights the following Cognitive Skills.

Summit Learning cognitive skills	
Argumentative claim	Developing a strong opinion/argument through clear, well-sequenced claims.
Informational/explanatory thesis	Constructing explanations or conveying ideas and information through clear, well-organized, relevant ideas.
Selection of evidence	Using relevant and sufficient evidence to support claims.
Explanation of evidence	Analyzing how the selected evidence supports the writer's statements (e.g., claims, controlling ideas).

C3 Framework Indicators

In addition to those noted in the Blueprint, this inquiry highlights the following C3 Framework indicators.

C3 Framework indicators
D2.Civ.10.6–8. Explain the relevance of personal interests and perspectives, civic virtues, and democratic principles when people address issues and problems in government and civil society. D2.Geo.4.6–8. Explain how cultural patterns and economic decisions influence environments and the daily lives of people in both nearby and distant places. D2.His.3.6–8. Use questions generated about individuals and groups to analyze why they, and the developments they shaped, are seen as historically significant. D2.His.14.6–8. Explain multiple causes and effects of events and developments in the past. D4.8.6–8. Apply a range of deliberative and democratic procedures to make decisions and take action in their classrooms and schools, and in out-of-school civic contexts.

Staging the Compelling Question

Staging the compelling question	
Compelling question	Why are reparations controversial?
Featured sources	**Source A:** "Ta-Nehisi Coates, Danny Glover, and Senator Cory Booker Speak at House Hearing on Reparations" (19 June 2019). Hearing in the House Judiciary regarding legislation on slavery reparations. NBC News. YouTube video. Accessed from: https://www.youtube.com/watch?v=bWZY-tSd1bs. **Source B:** "Reparations Move Deplored by Rustin" (9 May 1969). *New York Times*. Newspaper article. Accessed from: https://timesmachine.nytimes.com/timesmachine/1969/05/09/88992857.pdf.

The compelling question—*Why are reparations controversial?*—asks students to explore the tension surrounding discussions of race relations and reparations in the present day. To help students warm up for the inquiry, it is important to have them understand the term *reparations* and the various forms reparations can take. This discussion should prepare students to grapple with the controversy.

For the staging task, students generate questions surrounding the concept and forms of reparations. Teachers may need to share a dictionary definition to spark students' questioning. A question generation exercise could reflect the Question Formulation Technique (https://rightquestion. org/what-is-the-qft/). It may also entail prompting students to list as many questions as they can in a specified amount of time (e.g., three minutes) or listing the first five questions that come to mind. After students have generated questions, they should share their questions with classmates. This share-out can be in a Think-Pair-Share exercise, or be done as a whole-class discussion.

Once the staging task is completed, teachers can engage students in a discussion of instances where they think reparations are warranted. These examples can be small or large examples (i.e., impacting individuals or larger groups). Teachers may also prompt students to consider the ways in which individuals make amends to one another. Teachers should allow space for students to consider when/if they think reparations are appropriate on a conceptual level. Likewise, teachers should prompt students to consider the perspectives of people who may agree or disagree.

After completing the discussion, teachers may share the featured sources with students, asking them to consider the different perspectives in evidence. Likewise, teachers may choose to save the articles for a subsequent supporting question (e.g., supporting question 3 or 4).

Featured Sources

The following sources were selected to help introduce students to arguments for and against reparations. These sources help stage the inquiry, preparing students to engage in the inquiry process. Teachers should add/subtract, excerpt, modify, or annotate sources in order to respond to student needs.

Source A: This video is a clip from the House Judiciary hearing for legislation regarding slavery reparations. In the video, author Ta-Nehisi Coates, actor/activist Danny Glover, and Senator Cory Booker speak in support of reparations. Coates, in particular, has been a strong voice advocating on behalf of reparations. He is featured in a source for supporting question 3.

Source B: In an article from 1969, the *New York Times* reports civil rights leader Bayard Rustin's opposition to reparations. Rustin was a strong voice and strategist in the civil rights movement, influencing Martin Luther King Jr.'s nonviolent approach to civil disobedience.

Additional Source

Following is the "Black Manifesto," the speech from Jim Forman to which the *New York Times* article refers, delivered at the Riverside Church in New York City.

"Black Manifesto" (26 April 1969). *The Church Awakens: African Americans and the Struggle for Justice.* Accessed from: https://episcopalarchives.org /church-awakens/items/show/202.

What Makes "Equality" Equal?

Fourth- and Fifth-Grade Civil Rights Inquiry

Supporting Questions

1. Who fights for equality?
2. When is equality not equal?
3. How do laws change attitudes and behaviors?
4. How do attitudes and behaviors change laws?

	What makes "equality" equal?
C3 Framework indicators	D2.His.14.3–5. Explain probable causes and effects of events and developments. D2.His.16.3–5. Use evidence to develop a claim about the past. D2.Civ.4.3–5. Explain how groups of people make rules to create responsibilities and protect freedoms. D2.Civ.12.3–5. Explain how rules and laws change society and how people change rules and laws. D2.Civ.14.3–5. Illustrate historical and contemporary means of changing society.
Cognitive skills	Identifying patterns and relationships, synthesizing multiple sources
Staging the compelling question	Participate in a small-group discussion on this question: "Do we follow rules because we all already believe and do certain things, or do we believe and do certain things because they are rules?" Reference the list of classroom/school rules your teacher has written on the board.

Supporting question 1	Supporting question 2	Supporting question 3	Supporting question 4
Who fights for equality?	When is "equality" not equal?	How do laws change attitudes and behavior?	How do attitudes and behavior change laws?
Formative performance task	*Formative performance task*	*Formative performance task*	*Formative performance task*
Complete a graphic organizer that identifies groups who fought for social equality, their reasoning, and successful laws related to their civil rights.	Create an infographic defining the terms "legal equality" and "social reality."	Write a paragraph with examples from three rights movements describing how laws can change attitudes and behaviors.	Working collaboratively in small groups, construct a series of claims using evidence about how attitudes and behaviors change laws.

Featured sources	Featured sources	Featured sources	Featured sources
Source A: Video on civil rights movements **Source B:** Description of the Civil Rights Act (1964) **Source C:** Description of Nineteenth Amendment (1920) **Source D:** Description of *Obergefell v. Hodges* (2015)	**Source A:** US Constitution **Source B:** "Legal Equality and Social Reality Definitions" chart **Source C:** "How Laws Get Made" image **Source D:** List of evidence sources for social reality (opinion polls, media visibility, leadership visibility, hate crimes statistics)	**Source A:** "When Laws Change Minds" from *Psychology Today* **Source B:** "Affirmative Action" on Britannica Kids **Source C:** "Women's Rights" article describing Equal Pay Act and right to vote on Britannica Kids **Source D:** "Supreme Court Declares Marriage Equality for All 50 States," NPR	**Source A:** "Can New Rules Shape Public Opinion?" excerpt from *Psychology Today* **Source B:** "Affirmative Action Public Opinion," excerpt from Gallup **Source C:** Source providing evidence for social attitudes shifting law related to gender **Source D:** "Fifty Years Since Stonewall: The Change in Public Opinion," excerpt from *The Atlantic*

Summative performance task	**Argument:** What makes "equality" equal? Construct an argument that addresses the compelling question using specific claims and evidence. **Extension:** Create a visual representation of your argument to communicate your argument. This visual aid can be in the form of a PowerPoint, poster, etc.
Taking informed action	**Understand:** Review the class, school, or district rules. This evaluation can include the school/district handbook's policy on discrimination, harassment, or bullying. **Assess:** Evaluate whether the rules promote equality. **Act:** Draft a new or revised policy to propose. Or, if the policy/rules are adequate, create a schoolwide campaign to help other students better understand the policy.

Overview

Inquiry Description

This inquiry leads students through an investigation of legal equality (de jure equality) and social reality (de facto equality) in the context of three formative social justice movements: the civil rights movement, the women's rights movement, and the LGBT rights movement. By investigating the compelling question, "What makes 'equality' equal?" students examine the duality and reciprocity inherent within the concept of "equality" for historically marginalized groups. Historically marginalized groups have protested, raised awareness, and advocated to build social awareness and support in order to change laws. It is also true that marginalized groups have worked to change laws even when there was little public support, which helped to change public opinion. Students will come to understand that our understanding of equality is ever evolving, and that both laws (or rules) and social reality (majority group sentiment) can influence our shared definition of equality.

The formative performance tasks build on knowledge and skills through the course of the inquiry and help students understand that social change is an impetus for legal equality, and that law is an instrument of social change. Students create an evidence-based argument about whether legal equality or social reality is a more important driver for change in the context of US rights movements.

Students are invited to take informed action by examining their school rules or values around inclusion, and determine how they as a class can advance equality in their local school community. If students determine that the rules or principles advance equality, they may choose to influence the social realities in their community through an awareness campaign. If they determine that there are social realities that are not reflected in those rules, they may petition for appropriate changes.

This inquiry highlights the following standards:

- **History**
  - D2.His.14.3–5. Explain probable causes and effects of events and developments.
  - D2.His.16.3–5. Use evidence to develop a claim about the past.
- **Civics**
  - D2.Civ.4.3–5. Explain how groups of people make rules to create responsibilities and protect freedoms.
  - D2.Civ.12.3–5. Explain how rules and laws change society and how people change rules and laws.
  - D2.Civ.14.3–5. Illustrate historical and contemporary means of changing society.

Note: This inquiry is expected to take eight 30-minute class periods. The inquiry time frame could expand if teachers think their students need additional instructional experiences (e.g., supporting questions, formative performance tasks, featured sources, writing). Teachers are encouraged to adapt the inquiry to meet the needs and interests of their students. This inquiry lends itself to differentiation and modeling of historical thinking skills while assisting students in reading the variety of sources.

Structure of the Inquiry

In addressing the compelling question, "What makes 'equality' equal?" students work through a series of supporting questions, formative performance tasks, and featured sources in order to construct an argument supported by evidence while acknowledging competing perspectives.

Context of the Inquiry

This inquiry was developed through a collaboration between C3 Teachers and a team of Summit Learning curriculum fellows. This collection of inquiry projects was designed to meet the needs of states and districts, who are increasingly calling for ethnic and gender studies' inclusion in their school curriculums. Schools need culturally relevant materials that represent the histories and experiences of the communities they serve. The focus on culturally relevant curriculum is an inclusive focus. Culture is not a thing that some people have and others do not. This project, and others in the collection, represents a diverse set of identities and perspectives.

Cognitive Skills

The Summit Learning Cognitive Skills Rubric is an assessment and instruction tool that outlines the continuum of skills that are necessary for college and career readiness. Cognitive skills are interdisciplinary skills that require higher-order thinking and application.

The rubric includes thirty-six skills and eight score levels applicable to students in grades 3 through 12. Through Summit Learning, students practice and develop cognitive skills in every subject and in every grade level. The use of a common analytic rubric for assessment of project-based learning allows for targeted, standards-aligned feedback to students and supports the development of key skills over time. For more information, see the Cognitive Skills Rubric here: https://cdn.summitlearning.org/assets /marketing/Cognitive-Skills-Document-Suite.pdf.

The inquiry highlights the following cognitive skills:

Summit Learning cognitive skills	
Identifying patterns and relationships	Analyzing information to identify patterns and/or relationships relevant to understanding a phenomenon or to solve a design problem.
Synthesizing multiple sources	Integrating information across multiple sources to support an argument or explanation.

Staging the Compelling Question

To stage the compelling question, "What makes 'equality' equal?" teachers should generate with the class (or present students with) a list of classroom or school rules. Along with the compelling question, they should also present students with these two written staging questions:

- Do we follow rules because we already believe and do certain things?
- Or, do we believe and do certain things because they are rules?

This discussion frames the central part of the inquiry for students and situates it in terms of classroom and school rules, a type of "law" students are familiar with on an everyday basis. The discussion helps students understand that there is a cause-and-effect relationship between social attitudes and behaviors and the law. In some ways, we follow rules and laws because they are based on commonly held attitudes and accepted behaviors. In other ways, our attitudes and behaviors are shaped and changed by rules and laws. This sets students up for more detailed learning and application on this relationship after gaining context on the US rights movements.

How Can Communities Respond to Generational Trauma?

Eleventh-Grade US History Inquiry

Supporting Questions

1. Can a community carry trauma?
2. What are historical causes for generational trauma?
3. How have communities treated the effects of generational trauma?
4. How do communities respond to current, ongoing causes of trauma?

How can communities respond to generational trauma?	
C3 Framework indicators	**D2.Civ.5.9–12.** Evaluate citizens' and institutions' effectiveness in addressing social and political problems at the local, state, tribal, national, and/or international level. **D2.His.5.9–12.** Analyze how historical contexts shaped and continue to shape people's perspectives. **D2.His.15.9–12.** Distinguish between long-term causes and triggering effects in developing a historical argument.
Cognitive skills	Identifying patterns and relationships, making connections and inferences, argumentative claim
Staging the compelling question	Analyze lyrics from hip-hop artist and Pulitzer Prize winner Kendrick Lamar, making connections between historical causes of trauma and consequences to the Black community today.

Supporting question 1	*Supporting question 2*	*Supporting question 3*	*Supporting question 4*
Can a community carry trauma?	What are historical causes for generational trauma?	How have communities responded to the effects of generational trauma?	How do communities respond to current, ongoing causes of trauma?
Formative performance task	*Formative performance task*	*Formative performance task*	*Formative performance task*
Write a paragraph that describes generational trauma, including root causes, ways trauma can be transferred generationally, and effects of generational trauma on Black marginalized communities.	Using the provided template, create an outline that compares events from three different time periods that were the result of social injustices aimed at the Black community and the effects they had on society.	Write a review of an artistic work that represents the artist's perspective on accumulated fear and generational trauma in the Black community, citing both works and interviews.	Write an evidence-based claim about how current social justice movements are addressing causes of trauma to Black marginalized communities.

Featured sources	Featured sources	Featured sources	Featured sources
Source A: Excerpts from *The Legacy of Trauma* (APA, 2019) **Source B:** A definitional resource describing marginalization	**Source A:** "The Racist Roots of American Policing: From Slave Patrols to Traffic Stops," from *The Conversation,* June 2020 **Source B:** *Systemic Inequality: Displacement, Exclusion, and Segregation* (Center for American Progress, 2019)	**Source A:** Artist Gloria Swain uses art to cope, heal generational trauma **Source B:** "Artists Who Are Standing Against Racism and Police Brutality With Their Music Right Now," *Complex,* June 2020 **Source C:** "Art in the Face of Gentrification," *Shelterforce,* July 2017	**Source A:** "Meet the Young Activists Behind NY BLM Protests," *NY Magazine,* July 2020 **Source B:** Profile of an activist addressing economic oppression

Summative performance task	**Argument:** *How should communities respond to generational trauma?* Construct an argument in the form of an op-ed that addresses the compelling question, using specific claims and relevant evidence of responses to the effects of and causes of generational trauma.
	Extension: Create short, shareable digital media (zine or video clip) that represent ways Black artists and activists have responded and addressed generational trauma in their community.
Taking informed action	**Understand:** Study the impact that generational trauma has on Black marginalized communities and the consequences they carry from the past to the present. **Assess:** Analyze how artwork, music, or essays retell the story of generational trauma and accumulated fears in Black marginalized communities. **Act:** Write, record, and publish a podcast that profiles an artist or activist that is addressing injustices experienced by Black marginalized communities (much like the podcast *Dissect* does) in order to tell the public the true story of that artist, including their motivations, actions, and impact.

Overview
Inquiry Description

This inquiry introduces the concept of generational trauma and leads students through an investigation of social injustices to the Black community that have caused trauma. Students will investigate causes of trauma, ways trauma can be transferred from one generation to the next, and ways communities are responding to trauma. These include both ways communities can process generational trauma and ways that communities are responding to the ongoing social injustices that sustain generational trauma.

Students begin by developing an understanding of the dynamics of generational trauma and accumulated fear, and how these are transferred and perpetuated. Next, students will build an understanding of the root causes (including historical events and actions) of these intergenerational traumas. The two examples that will be presented are inequitable policing and unfair housing practices. Students will then be presented with artists who explore these themes in their works and hear artists' statements on ways the arts allow communities to heal from trauma. Students will also be presented with activists' responses to current injustices.

By exploring historical and contemporary injustices and a variety of ways communities respond, students will better understand the linkages between the need for communities to process or heal, and to take action against causes of generational trauma.

Note: This inquiry is expected to take fifteen 90-minute class periods. The inquiry time frame could expand if teachers think their students need additional instructional experiences (e.g., supporting questions, formative performance tasks, featured sources, writing). Teachers are encouraged to adapt the inquiry to meet the needs and interests of their students. This inquiry lends itself to differentiation and modeling of historical thinking skills while assisting students in reading a variety of sources.

Content Background

In 1865 when the Thirteenth Amendment was passed, officially abolishing slavery in the United States, Black Americans faced an uphill battle resulting in trauma and accumulated fears throughout the community. Starting soon after the Reconstruction policies of 1865 put in place by Congress to integrate 4 million newly freed slaves into the US, unofficial laws called "Black codes" started to take shape in the form of forced labor contracts toward freed slaves that, if refused, could lead to work without pay or arrest. In 1877 Jim Crow laws surfaced, enforcing racial segregation throughout the South for almost a century until the passing of the Civil Rights Act of 1964, outlawing, among other things, discrimination based on race. Even after this law was enacted, equal opportunities and fair treatment of African Americans was hardly enforced, leading to almost three centuries of countless social injustices aimed at disenfranchised Black marginalized communities throughout the US that still exist today. The question of how past and present social injustices impact modern society, and whether or not there is still a need for change, is the central focus of this inquiry.

It is important to note that this inquiry requires prerequisite knowledge and understanding of the following terms: social injustices, marginalized communities, generational trauma, and accumulated fears.

Structure of the Inquiry

This inquiry opens with two compelling questions that allow students to begin to analyze and consider the current state of social injustice in America as it is related to an important event of the past, Nat Turner's Rebellion, through the lens of a posthumous conversation between Kendrick Lamar and 2Pac Shakur. With this context in place, the inquiry then focuses on four supporting questions that start by building knowledge around the impact that generational trauma and accumulated fears have on marginalized communities, as well as the impact they hold on those who live within the community and society as a whole. The inquiry then shifts toward analyzing important social justice artists, activists, and movements, and determining their responsibility in educating and helping society process social injustices of the past and present.

In the summative task, students produce an argument in the form of an op-ed in response to the compelling question, "Do the injustices of the past contribute to the injustices of the present?" In addition, students will extend their learning by creating a multimedia presentation highlighting one of their areas of research. Finally, as a means to take an informed action, students will write and publish an original podcast that tells the true story of a social justice movement centered around an artist, musician, author, etc., in order to bring awareness to the public and help shift away from the traditional narrative that has been taught in schools for so long.

Staging the Compelling Question

This inquiry takes its inspiration from hip-hop artist Kendrick Lamar, the first artist of his genre to win the Pulitzer Prize for music (2018).

Much of Lamar's discography is an act of social justice that examines ongoing racial injustices in America and the struggles he himself faces through success, as he examines his past and the inescapable effects that generational trauma and accumulated fears hold over not only his life, but the lives of an entire marginalized community. His music is created to act as a voice for those who have otherwise been silenced through the teaching of a watered-down and inaccurate history in American schools. Speaking these truths through his music forces his listeners to consider the relationship between the social injustices of the past and present and the need for change in today's society.

Listen to the clip from season 5, episode 1 (24:00–34:13), of the podcast *Dissect*, in which Kendrick Lamar's album, *To Pimp a Butterfly*, is analyzed, and answer the following questions about Kendrick's conversation with 2Pac about the current injustices in America. As an additional resource, you may choose to listen to the song, "Mortal Man" from *To Pimp a Butterfly* to hear the conversation in full.

1. What does 2Pac mean when he says, "The ground is going to open and swallow the people?" Do you agree or disagree with this statement?

2. 2Pac then says, "Next time there is a riot, there is going to be bloodshed. It's going to be Nat Turner 1831." The podcast then goes on to explain Nat Turner's Rebellion, including the causes and consequences. Based on the information you've gathered and what you know about injustices in America today, do you feel there is truth to 2Pac's statement? Why or why not?

What Does the Way a Nation Treats Immigrants Say About Its Leaders?

Sixth- to Eighth-Grade Inquiry

Supporting Questions

1. What was the message and impact of Ashama's policy toward refugees?
2. To what extent do contemporary leaders reflect Ashama's "pastoral care"?
3. How do local leaders reflect Ashama's "pastoral care"?

What does the way a nation treats immigrants say about its leaders?

C3 Framework indicators	**D2.Civ.1.6–8.** Distinguish the powers and responsibilities of citizens, political parties, interest groups, and the media in a variety of governmental and nongovernmental contexts. **D2.Geo.10.6–8.** Analyze the ways in which cultural and environmental characteristics vary among various regions of the world. **D2.His.1.6–8.** Analyze connections among events and developments in broader historical contexts.
Cognitive skills	Synthesizing multiple sources, argumentative claim, comparing and contrasting
Staging the compelling question	Students construct a class definition of the concept *pastoral care*.

Supporting question 1	*Supporting question 2*	*Supporting question 3*
What was the message of Ashama's policy toward refugees?	How do contemporary leaders reflect Ashama's "pastoral care"?	To what extent can local leaders reflect Ashama's "pastoral care"?
Formative performance task	*Formative performance task*	*Formative performance task*
Analyze speeches and documents detailing local indigenous deliberations to determine King Ashama's beliefs and values about refugee communities.	Analyze Boris Johnson's and Donald Trump's beliefs statements about refugee communities in speeches or statements.	Identify the role of nongovernmental/community-driven leadership to support refugee communities.
Featured sources	*Featured sources*	*Featured sources*
Source A: Interview with Dr. Michael Ralph on King Ashama, pastoral care, and community deliberations **Source B:** *A History of Ethiopia* **Source C:** *The Life of Muhammad*	**Source A:** "Boris Johnson Is Shutting the Door on Child Refugees," Foreign Policy **Source B:** "Trump Cuts Refugee Cap…" *Washington Post* **Source C:** "World leaders voice strong support for new refugee deal…," United Nations High Commissioner for Refugees	**Source A:** "The History of South Central LA," KCET, 2017 **Source B:** "How Nipsey Hussle Connected with his Eritrean Roots," CNN, 2019 **Source C:** "Remembering Nipsey Hussle, Cultural and Community Activist Extraordinaire," *NonProfit Quarterly*, 2019 **Source D:** "Nipsey Hussle's Work for the Black Community Went Deeper Than You Think," HuffPost, 2019

Summative performance task	**Argument:** How can leaders care for refugees? Construct an argument (e.g., detailed outline, poster, essay) that evaluates the way leaders care for refugees, using a lens of "pastoral care." Use specific claims and relevant evidence from historical and contemporary sources, while acknowledging competing views.
	Extension: Engage in a local indigenous deliberation (public deliberation) about policies towards refugee/immigrant communities.
Taking informed action	**Understand:** Learn about the social and political challenges facing refugees in your local community as well as the ways in which communities are addressing their own challenges (by connecting with a local immigration center, collecting stories from the community, and the like). **Assess:** Evaluate current actions and determine ways in which leaders can support one or more of the challenges identified. **Act:** Create a presentation to a leader of your choosing and advocate for a policy that would address a challenge local refugees are facing.

Overview
Inquiry Description

This inquiry leads students through an investigation of how leaders, past and present, respond to the needs of refugee communities. Using a lens of "pastoral care" across lines of difference, students explore values-based leadership, considering the resulting social and political outcomes for national (or global) communities. Beginning with King Ashama (in the 7th century Kingdom of Aksum), students examine a historical example of a national leader extending compassion to a refugee community, demonstrating a recognition of unity and humanity across lines of difference. Next, students examine contemporary examples of national leaders who do/don't demonstrate care to refugee or immigrant communities. To close the inquiry, students consider how local leaders (whether well-known or lesser-known individuals) can also demonstrate pastoral care. An activist whose father was an Eritrean refugee, Nipsey Hussle, is featured. By connecting a historical example to a modern context, students are using world history to construct an argument and take action around the compelling question: *How can leaders care for refugees?*

In this inquiry, students consider how leaders' understanding of *care* and *community*—whether at the local, national, or global level—manifests in policies. Likewise, students consider how fairness, justice, and humanity are at the core of these policy decisions.

Structure of the Inquiry

In addressing the compelling question—*How can leaders care for refugees?*—students work through a series of supporting questions, formative performance tasks, and featured sources in order to construct an argument supported by evidence and counterevidence from a variety of sources.

Note: This inquiry is expected to take eight 30-minute class periods. The inquiry time frame could expand if teachers think their students need additional instructional experiences (e.g., supporting questions, formative performance tasks, featured sources, writing). Teachers are encouraged to adapt the inquiry to meet the needs and interests of their students. This inquiry lends itself to differentiation and modeling of historical thinking skills while assisting students in reading the variety of sources.

Context of the Inquiry

This inquiry was developed through a collaboration between C3 Teachers and a team of Summit Learning curriculum fellows. This collection of inquiry projects was designed to meet the needs of states and districts, who are increasingly calling for ethnic and gender studies' inclusion in curriculum. Schools need culturally relevant materials that represent the histories and experiences of the communities they serve. The focus on culturally relevant curriculum is an inclusive focus. Culture is not a thing that some people have and others do not. This project, and others in the collection, represents a diverse set of identities and perspectives.

Content Background

Kingdom of Aksum. This inquiry bridges content about 7th-century Aksum king, Ashama, with modern leaders. The African Kingdom of Aksum (Axum), 1st–8th centuries CE, spanned the horn of Africa, encompassing areas of modern-day Eritrea, Ethiopia, Somalia, Somaliland, and Djibouti. It would eventually form the Kingdom of Abyssinia in the 13th century. Aksum expanded its influence through trade, possessing a strong agricultural economy. It was one of the first states in the world to adopt Christianity; it was the first to adopt it on the African continent. The inquiry is framed by the connection of the Ashama's pastoral care to modern-day responses to refugees, particularly considering the connection to Eritrean history and identity.

Abrahamic Faiths. Prior to this inquiry, students should have some experience with the African kingdoms, as well as some basic knowledge of the histories of the three Abrahamic faiths (i.e., Judaism, Christianity, Islam). The connection between the religions is referenced in a Featured Source from Supporting Question 1.

As noted in the staging sources, *pastoral care* has religious roots, but encapsulates an understanding of care that is not tied to any one religion. Regardless, teachers should be conscientious about framing *pastoral care* as an analytical lens for this particular history and its contemporary applications.

Naming Convention. The source information in Supporting Question 1 contains different names and terms for different places and people. For example, Ashama is referenced in many different ways. His full name is Ashama ibn-Abjar, but is often referred to simply as "the Negus"—Negus being a royal title for someone in the Ethiopian Semitic language. In Arabic, "Negus" is "al-Najashi." In one of the sources, it is spelled "Nagāshī." To support students' comprehension, names were changed to "Ashama" for consistency and clarity.

Other names were changed to reflect modern conventions. For example, the "Ḳoraish" tribe was changed to "Quraysh."

Cognitive Skills

The Summit Learning Cognitive Skills Rubric is an assessment and instruction tool that outlines the continuum of skills that are necessary for college and career readiness. Cognitive skills are interdisciplinary skills that require higher-order thinking and application.

The rubric includes thirty-six skills and eight score levels applicable to students in grades 3 through 12. Through Summit Learning, students practice and develop cognitive skills in every subject and in every grade level. The use of a common analytic rubric for assessment of project-based learning allows for targeted, standards-aligned feedback to students and supports the development of key skills over time. For more information, see the Cognitive Skills Rubric here: https://cdn.summitlearning.org /assets/marketing/Cognitive-Skills-Document-Suite.pdf.

The inquiry highlights the following cognitive skills:

Summit Learning cognitive skills	
Identifying patterns and relationships	Analyzing information to identify patterns and/or relationships relevant to understanding a phenomenon or to solve a design problem.
Synthesizing multiple sources	Integrating information across multiple sources to support an argument or explanation.

Staging the Compelling Question

Staging the compelling question	
Compelling question	How can leaders care for refugees?
Staging task	Students construct a class definition of the concept *pastoral care*.

To stage the compelling question and inquiry, students construct a class definition of the concept *pastoral care*. This concept provides the analytical frame of the inquiry.

Teachers could begin this task by having students first generate ideas around the term *care*. Their idea generation can be through a list or word web, and likewise can be performed individually or as a group. Teachers should encourage students to think about *care* in terms of people, actions, ideas, feelings, and the like. Next, students should define *pastoral*, which can include using a dictionary definition. Teachers might then ask students how that adjective may change the meaning of *care*. After this initial conversation, teachers could have students read one (or more) of the provided excerpts on pastoral care. Using each other's explanation, students should compare and contrast the ideas with their own initial definitions. Synthesizing students' initial work and the sources, the class constructs a definition of *pastoral care*.

Featured Sources

The following sources were selected to provide students with different, but complementary, definitions of pastoral care. These sources can help students create a more nuanced understanding of *care* and *pastoral care*. All three excerpts come from a collection of articles on pastoral care: Kujawa-Holbrook's *Injustice and the Care of Souls: Taking Oppression Seriously in Pastoral Care* (Fortress Press, 2009). Teachers should add or delete, excerpt, modify, or annotate sources in order to respond to student needs.

As these pieces are written for more academic audiences, teachers are encouraged to modify the sources and/or provide word banks to support student needs. An initial word bank is provided. Teachers should add additional terms, if needed.

Source A explains pastoral care in terms of Muslim communities in the United States.

Source B describes pastoral care around ideas of love and power, noting the importance of taking an antiracist stance in pastoral care.

Source C doesn't reference the term "pastoral" care, but rather looks at care through a lens of "practical solidarity."

Staging the Compelling Question

Staging the compelling question

Featured source A	Kobeisy, A. N. M. (2009). "Light at the End of the Tunnel: Pastoral Care for Muslims," in *Injustice and the Care of Souls: Taking Oppression Seriously in Pastoral Care*, ed. Sheryl Kujawa-Holbrook. Minneapolis: Fortress Press, 103, 105–6, 122 (excerpt).

The United States is a microcosm of humanity. No other country has a greater diversity of races, ethnic, cultural, and religious groups. Although the United States offers a great asylum for diverse people, cultures are always encouraged to assimilate and even disappear into what is called the "melting pot." . . .

It is the consensus of Muslim scholars, as well as scholars of other faiths and societies, that the Muslim community is little understood, and is underserved in the United States. Unfair treatment of Muslims in the United States has damaged and continues to threaten the mental health of American Muslims. . . .

In this time and age of increasing diversity and rapid globalization, there is no excuse for not properly, accurately, and sensitively understanding and serving each other with dignity.

Word Bank

Microcosm: A small place that captures the characteristics of something larger; in this case, the United States is representative of all of humanity because of its diversity.

Assimilate: To absorb and bring in people, ideas, or culture into a wider society.

Laypeople: Nonordained members of a church.

Globalization: The process of global interaction and connections between people, organizations, and governments.

Staging the Compelling Question

Staging the compelling question
Featured source B   Kujawa-Holbrook, S. A. (2009). "Love and Power: Antiracist Pastoral Care," in *Injustice and the Care of Souls: Taking Oppression Seriously in Pastoral Care*, ed. Sheryl Kujawa-Holbrook. Minneapolis: Fortress Press, 13–4 (excerpt).

> . . . *power without love is reckless and abusive, and love without power is sentimental and anemic. Power at its best is love implementing the demands of justice, and justice at its best is power correcting everything that stands against love.*
>
> —Martin Luther King Jr. (1967)*

When Dr. [Martin Luther] King spoke of love and power, he was talking about the "connective tissue" that holds together all of the human community. As the stories from the articles featured in this book suggest, pastoral care that recognizes the realities of oppression is also an exercise in love and power. . . .

Love and power transform pastoral care and make an impact on the larger human community. One of the reasons so many attempts at pastoral care fail to bring authentic healing and reconciliation is that the overall dominant culture within American society often does not recognize or strive to correct the deep power imbalances experienced by all marginalized people. Antiracist pastoral care emanates from the collective concern

---

*King, Martin Luther Jr. 1967. "Where Do We Go from Here?" Annual Report Delivered at the 11th Convention of the Southern Christian Leadership Conference, August 16, Atlanta, GA. (Excerpts).

that we are all, despite the divisions we perpetuate, part of one human community; if life is improved for one person, all benefit.

Word Bank

Reconciliation: Action of restoring (bringing back) friendly relations.

Strive: Make great effort to achieve something.

Marginalize: To treat people as insignificant or decentered.

Emanate: Originate from, produced by.

Perpetuate: Make something continue.

Staging the Compelling Question

Staging the compelling question	
Featured source C	Gill-Austern, B. I. (2009). "Engaging Diversity and Difference: From Practices of Exclusion to Practices of Practical Solidarity," in *Injustice and the Care of Souls: Taking Oppression Seriously in Pastoral Care*, ed. Sheryl Kujawa-Holbrook. Minneapolis: Fortress Press, 33, 40 (excerpt).

This excerpt does not reference "pastoral" care, but rather, looks at pastoral care through the lens of practical solidarity.

. . . pastoral care is faithful living by finite creatures in their particular historical context. Our particular historical context demands that we give increased attention to the exclusion practiced through abandonment by the "haves" and the "have-nots" of our world. How can one billion people, almost one-fifth of the world's population, live on less than a dollar a day unless much of the world simply accepts their fate with indifference and abandons them to their plight? . . .

We never fully know home until we have left it, until we have made a pilgrimage to somewhere else. . . . Pilgrimage becomes a way to deconstruct the home that has built borders to keep others out, as well as to see clearly where it has created space to receive others. If we are not careful we can slip into the exclusion of assimilation, coming to see the "other" only through our own lens, instead of getting ourselves a new set of glasses. . . .

To overcome the practices of exclusion that undergird oppression we need to find ways to weave ties of connection and relationship with those outside of whatever we call home.

Word Bank

Finite: Having limits, restrictions.

Exclusion: To reject, prohibit, keep someone from being included.

Pilgrimage: A religious journey.

Undergird: Provide support or a firm basis.

Assimilation: To absorb and bring in people, ideas, or culture into a wider society.

Notes

Introduction

1. Django Paris, "Culturally Sustaining Pedagogy: A Needed Change in Stance, Terminology, and Practice," *Educational Researcher* 41, no. 3 (2012): 93–7, https://doi.org/10.3102/0013189X12441244.

Chapter 1

1. Prentice Chandler and Douglas McKnight, "Race and Social Studies," in *Contemporary Social Studies: An Essential Reader*, ed. William Benedict Russell III (Charlotte, NC: Information Age Publishing, 2011), 215–42; Geneva Gay, "The Importance of Multicultural Education," in *The Curriculum Studies Reader*, 2nd edition, ed. David J. Flinders and Stephen J. Thornton (New York: RoutledgeFalmer, 2004): 315–20; Gloria Ladson-Billings, "Lies My Teacher Still Tells: Developing a Critical Race Perspective Toward the Social Studies," in *Critical Race Theories Perspectives on the Social Studies: The Profession, Policies, and Curriculum*, ed. Gloria Ladson-Billings (Charlotte, NC: Information Age Publishing, 2003), 1–11.
2. Peggy McIntosh, "White Privilege and Male Privilege: A Personal Account of Coming to See Correspondences Through Work in Women's Studies," in *Race, Class & Gender: An Anthology*, ed. Margaret L. Andersen and Patricia Hill Collins (Belmont, CA: Wadsworth, 1988), 95–105; Robin DiAngelo, *White Fragility: Why It's So Hard for White People to Talk About Racism* (Boston: Beacon Press, 2018).
3. Gloria Ladson-Billings, "Toward a Theory of Culturally Relevant Pedagogy," *American Educational Research Journal* 32, no. 3 (1995): 469.
4. Ladson-Billings, "Lies," 4.
5. Geneva Gay, "Preparing for Culturally Responsive Teaching," *Journal of Teacher Education* 53, no. 2 (2002): 106–16.
6. Gloria Ladson-Billings, "Culturally Relevant Pedagogy 2.0: a.k.a. the Remix," *Harvard Educational Review* 84, no. 1 (2014): 74–84.
7. Kadhir Rajagopal, *Create Success! Unlocking the Potential of Urban Students* (Alexandria, VA: ASCD, 2011), 26–7.
8. Angela Valenzuela and Brenda Rubio, "Subtractive Schooling," in *The TESOL Encyclopedia of English Language Teaching*, ed. John I. Liontas (Hoboken, NJ: John Wiley & Sons, 2018), 4356–62.

9. Gloria Ladson-Billings, "Toward a Theory," 476.
10. Matthew M. Chingos and Grover J. "Russ" Whitehurst, *Choosing Blindly: Instructional Materials, Teacher Effectiveness, and the Common Core* (Washington, DC: Brookings Institution, 2012); Linda Darling-Hammonds, Maria E. Hyler, and Madelyn Gardner, *Effective Teacher Professional Development* (Palo Alto, CA, and Washington, DC: Learning Policy Institute, 2017).
11. Ladson-Billings, "Culturally Relevant Pedagogy 2.0," 76.
12. Django Paris, "Culturally Sustaining Pedagogy: A Needed Change in Stance, Terminology, and Practice," *Educational Researcher* 41, no. 3 (2012): 93–7, https://doi.org/10.3102/0013189X12441244.
13. Luis C. Moll et al., "Funds of Knowledge for Teaching: Using a Qualitative Approach to Connect Homes and Classrooms," *Theory into Practice* 31, no. 2 (1992): 132–41.
14. Christopher L. Busey and William B. Russell III, "'We Want to Learn': Middle School Latino/a Students Discuss Social Studies Curriculum and Pedagogy," *RMLE Online* 39, no. 4 (2016): 1–20.
15. Ladson-Billings, "Lies," 4.
16. Virginia Kay Williams and Nancy Deyoe, "Diverse Population, Diverse Collection? Youth Collections in the United States," *Technical Services Quarterly* 31, no. 2 (2014): 97–121.

Chapter 2

1. Fred Paas, Alexander Renkl, and John Sweller, "Cognitive Load Theory and Instructional Design: Recent Developments," *Educational Psychologist* 38, no. 1 (2003): 1–4.
2. Christine E. Sleeter, *The Academic and Social Value of Ethnic Studies* (Washington, DC: National Education Association, 2011).
3. Allyson Tintiangco-Cubales et al., "Toward an Ethnic Studies Pedagogy: Implications for K–12 Schools from the Research," *The Urban Review* 47, no. 1 (2015): 104–25.
4. Gloria Ladson-Billings, "Toward a Theory of Culturally Relevant Pedagogy," *American Educational Research Journal* 32, no. 3 (1995): 465–91; Christopher Busey and William B. Russell III, "'We Want to Learn': Middle School Latino/a Students Discuss Social Studies Curriculum and Pedagogy," *RMLE Online* 39, no. 4 (2016): 1–20.
5. Rudine Sims Bishop, "Mirrors, Windows, and Sliding Glass Doors," *Perspectives* 6 no. 3 (1990).

Chapter 3

1. Gloria Ladson-Billings, "Lies My Teacher Still Tells: Developing a Critical Race Perspective Toward the Social Studies," in *Critical Race Theories Perspectives on the Social Studies: The Profession, Policies, and Curriculum*, ed. Gloria Ladson-Billings (Charlotte, NC: Information Age Publishing, 2003), 1–11.
2. Jeffrey Alan Ellison, "How They Teach the Holocaust in Jewish Day Schools," *Cogent Education* 4, no. 1 (2017).

Chapter 4

1. Jay McTighe and Grant P. Wiggins, *Essential Questions: Opening Doors to Student Understanding* (Alexandria, VA: ASCD, 2013).

2. S. G. Grant, John Lee, and Kathy Swan Grant, *Inquiry-Based Practice in Social Studies Education: Understanding the Inquiry Design Model* (New York: Routledge, 2017).

Chapter 5

1. ReLeah Cossett Lent, *Overcoming Textbook Fatigue: 21st Century Tools to Revitalize Teaching and Learning* (Alexandria, VA: ASCD, 2012), 4–6.
2. Donna Recht and Lauren Leslie, "Effect of Prior Knowledge on Good and Poor Readers' Memory of Text," *Journal of Educational Psychology* 80, no. 1 (1988): 16.
3. Anthony De Jesús and René Antrop-González, "Instrumental Relationships and High Expectations: Exploring Critical Care in Two Latino Community-Based Schools," *Intercultural Education* 17, no. 3 (2006): 281–99.
4. Christine Sleeter, *The Academic and Social Value of Ethnic Studies* (Washington, DC: National Education Association, 2011), 8–9.
5. Angela Valenzuela and Brenda Rubio, "Subtractive Schooling," in *The TESOL Encyclopedia of English Language Teaching*, ed. John I. Liontas (Hoboken, NJ: John Wiley & Sons, 2018), 4356–62.
6. J. M. Vasquez, "Ethnic Identity and Chicano Literature: How Ethnicity Affects Reading and Reading Affects Ethnic Consciousness," *Ethnic and Racial Studies* 28, no. 5 (2005): 913–14.

Chapter 6

1. Vershawn Ashanti Young, "'Nah, We Straight': An Argument Against Code Switching," *JAC* 29, no. 1/2 (2009): 49–76.
2. Martha Tesema, "A Beginner's Guide to Taking Up Space," *Shine*, July 20, 2020, https://advice.shinetext.com/articles/a-beginners-guide-to-taking-up-space/.
3. Marcela Cuellar, "The Impact of Hispanic-Serving Institutions (HSIs), Emerging HSIs, and Non-HSIs on Latina/o Academic Self-Concept," *Review of Higher Education* 37, no. 4 (2014): 499–520.
4. Keith Miller, "Epistemology of a Drum Major: Martin Luther King, Jr. and the Black Folk Pulpit," *Rhetoric Society Quarterly* 18, no. 3–4 (1988): 225–36.
5. Harald Klinke, ed., *Art Theory as Visual Epistemology* (Newcastle Upon Tyne, UK: Cambridge Scholars Publishing, 2014).

Chapter 7

1. Heidi Hayes Jacobs, *Interdisciplinary Curriculum: Design and Implementation* (Alexandria, VA: ASCD, 1989), 8–10.
2. Barbara Moss et al., *A Close Look at Close Reading: Teaching Students to Analyze Complex Texts, Grades 6–12* (Alexandria, VA: ASCD, 2015), 47–58.
3. Norman L. Webb, "Depth-of-Knowledge Levels for Four Content Areas" (unpublished paper), March 28, 2002.

Chapter 8

1. Conference on College Composition and Communication, *Students' Right to Their Own Language* (Urbana, IL: National Council of Teachers of English, 1974).
2. Geneva Gay, *Culturally Responsive Teaching: Theory, Research, and Practice* (New York: Teachers College Press, 2018), 218–19.
3. Martin Nystrand et al., *Opening Dialogue* (New York: Teachers College Press, 1997).

Chapter 9

1. Sylvia A Morelli, Matthew D. Lieberman, and Jamil Zaki, "The Emerging Study of Positive Empathy," *Social and Personality Psychology Compass* 9, no. 2 (2015): 57–68.
2. Kimberly S. Adams and Sandra L. Christenson, "Differences in Parent and Teacher Trust Levels: Implications for Creating Collaborative Family-School Relationships," *Special Services in the Schools* 14, no. 1–2 (1998): 1–22.
3. Chau-kiu Cheung and Raymond Kwok-hong Chan, "Social Capital as Exchange: Its Contribution to Morale," *Social Indicators Research* 96, no. 2 (2010): 205–27.

About the Author

Evan Gutierrez serves as the Managing Director for Curriculum and Assessment for Gradient Learning. Gutierrez fosters innovation in curriculum and program design through collaborative partnerships with a focus on advancing equity. Prior to joining Gradient, he oversaw the academic program for Acero Schools in Chicago, a high performing charter network serving the Latino community. He has engaged in course, program, and school model design with school districts and charter management organizations in Los Angeles, Chicago, New York City, and New Orleans. Gutierrez graduated with a BA in Jazz Performance from Berklee College of Music, and an MBA with additional graduate study in Curriculum and Instruction from Loyola Marymount University. He lives in Michigan with his wife, April, and children, Silvio and Miriam.

Acknowledgments

The work that this book represents has spanned years. It also has been made possible because people invested in the idea first, then the work, even when there was less clarity and public support than there is at present. I have been supported, nudged, challenged, and celebrated by many dozens of people along the way. The following are my special thanks to the people who have made this work and book possible.

First, I want to thank my wife and best friend, April Gutierrez, a constant source of inspiration and most of my good ideas. Thanks to my children for giving me the conviction to push for change, and tolerating countless refrains of "papa is working," as much of this book was written during quarantine. Thanks to my parents for teaching me how to be a good human, and how to think.

Thanks to leaders who supported this work before it was a thing. These include Shawn Rubin, Andrew Goldin, and Dr. John Lee.

Thanks to the designers whose work is featured in this book, for not only creating great curriculum but also sharing their thought process along the way: David Alfafara, Malika Ali, Annabeth Edens, Cam Lloyd, and Ericka Streeter-Adams. Thanks to the scholars that accompanied them in their work: Michael Bronski, Johanna Eager, Dr. Michael Ralph, Dr. Shantá R. Robinson, Dr. Yohuru Williams, Dr. Benjamin Fitzpatrick, and Nina Louise Alsbrook. Thanks to Dr. Carly Muetterties for her tireless and expert work in supporting the above.

Gratitude to the Acero Schools team that pioneered this work and helped to lay a firm foundation, particularly those whose work is featured here: Tim Croel, Mary O'Brien-Combs, Nataly Lopez-Diaz, and Muriel Ortiz.

Index